Love Those Red Sox

One Man's Baseball Journey

by EJ Barney

Love Those Red Sox

One Man's Baseball Journey

by EJ Barney

Railroad Street Press
394 Railroad Street, Suite 2
St. Johnsbury, VT 05819

All rights reserved by the author. No parts of this book may be copied or reproduced without the express written consent of the author.

Published in the United States by Railroad Street Press,
St. Johnsbury, Vermont.

ISBN: 9781936711000

Library of Congress Control Number
2010918035
1. Memoir

Jacket design by Susanna V. Walden.

First Edition 2011

Railroad Street Press
394 Railroad Street, Suite 2
St. Johnsbury, VT 05819
(802) 748-3551
www.railroadstreetpress.com

INTRODUCTION

In the pages that follow, you will meet an extraordinary lady who knew all about life and a little bit about baseball. Joanne thought the New York Yankees and Brooklyn Dodgers played in the World Series every year. She believed in her husband's ability to finish the story they started in 1991 when they thought the Red Sox were going to win the World Series. In 2010, the two of us traveled to Vermont, to the heart of Red Sox country. We rented a condominium in East Burke and life was good.

In St. Johnsbury, my hometown, we met Amy Nixon and Tina Keach, two incredibly talented and ambitious women who were destined to play a major role in helping to bring our amazing story to fruition.

On June 1st, 2010, the Caledonian-Record of St. Johnsbury published the interview Amy Nixon had conducted with me at the condo. Meanwhile, Tina Keach, the manager of the local Elks Club arranged to have me give a presentation about my Red Sox experiences which would coincide with the kickoff for the Relay For Life, an annual event to raise money for the American Cancer Society. It was noteworthy because I am a cancer survivor, defeating Non-Hodgkins Lymphoma in 2003. Joanne and her fourteen year old grandson, Jacob, were there, as were Arnie and Winona Gadapee from Danville, Vermont where Arnie and I graduated from Danville High School in 1954.

Joanne beamed with pride as she listened to her husband talk about his amazing survival stories, including recovery from a five way bypass in 1992, having both carotid arteries operated on in 1996, beating the cancer in 2003 and suffering three heart attacks between 2005 and 2008. In 2007, doctors at a Las Vegas hospital were performing a routine procedure on me, replacing a pacemaker with a combination pacemaker/defibrillator. They were preparing to test the device when my blood pressure dropped to zero and all electrical activity in my body ceased for two minutes. I awoke to find an intubator in my mouth and I wondered what had happened. When the doctors told me, I thanked them for bringing him back. "No, Mr. Barney, you brought yourself back," one of the doctors told me.

On July 30th, Joanne Barney became ill while eating lunch. A CT scan revealed bleeding in the back of the brain, in the cerebellum region. She was rushed to Dartmouth-Hitchcock Medical Center in Lebanon, New Hampshire where she underwent three hours of brain surgery. Doctors told me that the surgery was a success. I was elated, but sadly, she never regained consciousness and on Monday, August 2nd, 2010, Joanne's three daughters and I agreed that she should be disconnected from the ventilator. It was a heartbreaking decision, but also the right one. She passed away peacefully about an hour later.

This story is dedicated to my beautiful wife of 22 years. I loved her with all my heart and I could not have written this story without her. Oh yes, you will also meet an extraordinary Lynx point Siamese cat named Caspar who had the same kind of cancer that I had. How amazing is that?

The book is also dedicated to three of the greatest players ever to wear a Red Sox uniform, Ted Williams, Johnny Pesky and Bobby Doer.

This book has taken on a life of its own since its inception in 1990. The tale began as a rebuttal to Dan Shaughnessy's entertaining story about the alleged "Curse of The Bambino." The Red Sox had not won a World Series since 1918. There's no proof that the Babe ever said the Red Sox would never win another World Series. As a matter of fact, Ruth was a ballplayer who loved parties, nightlife, good food and the ladies. He was probably thrilled at the prospect of playing in New York City. He thrived on the media coverage. The Yankees knew how to win pennants. The Boston Red Sox, without Babe Ruth, didn't have a clue. And the Red Sox have certainly had their share of misfortunes over the years. I had suffered through so many disappointing endings to what should have been seasons when the ball club played good enough to win, only to lose because of an error or a bloop home run or some kind of nightmarish ending that nobody could have conceived. I was saddened as a nine year old kid in North Danville, Vermont, listening to the radio in Ray and Jean Locke's general store. There were no TV sets. We relied on our imaginations. Rodney Daniels was my next door neighbor and he was a St. Louis Cardinal fan. He liked Stan Musial. I liked Ted Williams. Stan and the Cards won the Series in seven games. I was brokenhearted in 1948 when my dad and I attended the first playoff game in the history of the American League. It was being played in Fenway Park and the Red Sox were heavily favored to beat the Cleveland Indians. My father had secured two tickets from a scalper the day before, after a doubleheader against the Yankees. Detroit beat Cleveland and the Fenway Park P.A. Announcer said: "Tickets for tomorrow's playoff game will go on sale immediately following this game." Jersey Street, now Yawkey Way, was a madhouse, chaotic scene. My father had my cousin Franklin take my brother and me back to the Statler Hotel while he stayed to get tickets. He showed up at the hotel hours later with his shirt ripped and his necktie gone, but he had two tickets in his hand, obtained at $20 apiece from a scalper. We were so excited and so sure the Red Sox were going to the World Series and play the Boston Braves. We had seats behind home plate and I remember seeing many of the Boston Braves players at the ballpark to scout the teams. The Braves had a couple of pitchers named Warren Spahn and Johnny Sain, two of the best in the National League. All of New England anticipated a Boston vs. Boston World Series. Alas, it wasn't to be. I remember looking up at the press box at Fenway Park and wishing I could be up there. Amazingly enough, I made that wish come true forty-three years later.

One

When the Boston Red Sox won the 2004 World Series, they erased eighty-six years of frustration. Additionally, they exorcised the so-called "Curse of The Bambino," allegedly created when George Herman "Babe" Ruth was unceremoniously sold to the rival New York Yankees in 1920. Ruth was a major star in Boston. Prior to 1920, he helped the team win five world championships. Was there really a curse on the team? Was it created when Ruth allegedly uttered those fateful words: "You guys will never win another World Series."

Dan Shaughnessy of the Boston Globe wrote "The Curse Of The Bambino" in 1990. I was working as a radio broadcaster at KSAY- FM located in Fort Bragg, California on the incredibly beautiful Mendocino coast of northern California. I had wanted to be involved with the Red Sox in some way since I was growing up in North Danville, Vermont. Every player on the team was a hero in my eyes. Now, more than forty-two years later, I was part of a radio program that would allow me to become involved with the Red Sox in ways I had only daydreamed about in Vermont and in Fenway Park.

My lovely wife, Joanne, and I were sharing a large upstairs studio apartment just south of Fort Bragg, across the highway from the Pine Beach Inn. The vast blue Pacific Ocean was less than a mile away from us and at night the sounds of the roaring surf would lull us to sleep.

I did not believe there was a curse on the team. I had related many

Boston baseball horror stories to Joanne since our marriage on a boat at Lake Tahoe, California/Nevada in July, 1988. She felt strongly that the fans' negative attitudes were bringing the Red Sox down every year. "They expect them to lose and they fulfill their worst expectations. The fans have been suffering for so many years."

I believed that my Red Sox heroes from the past needed to be recognized and honored for their contributions to the game. I was writing what I knew about Ted Williams, Johnny Pesky, Dominic DiMaggio, Bobby Doerr and other great Red Sox players using a big noisy word processor that printed out the page after the words were keyed on to the screen. My writing was clumsy and very disjointed and was going nowhere until Joanne made a suggestion. "Honey," she said. "If you really want to write about the Red Sox, then you need to go where they are." A light bulb came on in my head just like the comic book characters. What a great idea! 1991, coincidentally, was the fiftieth anniversary of Ted Williams hitting .406. Perhaps, I theorized if all the planets were in alignment and the ball took all the right bounces, this could be the year when the Red Sox would win it all.

It was February, 1991. The Red Sox were preparing for the season in Winter Haven, Florida. At the same time, I was honored to have Hall of Famer Bobby Doerr as a radio guest from his home in Junction City, Oregon. Bobby played second base for the Red Sox from 1937 to 1951 when back problems forced him into early retirement from baseball. He was elected to the National Baseball Hall of Fame in 1986 and his number "1" is retired at Fenway Park. I told him I wanted to write a story that would honor the great players like himself and disavow the so called curse. Bobby agreed that would be a good thing. Joanne didn't believe I was serious about the project until I gave my two week notice to the owner of KSAY. I was motivated and I was excited about the future. We made plans to drive to Florida in our little Dodge Colt with the advertising for the "Human Touch School of Therapeutic Massage" on the side of the front doors. We would be accompanied by our beautiful Lynx-point Siamese cat named Caspar. He loved riding in the car with us and he would prove to be a delightful traveling companion.

Joanne and I were taking a risk, a leap of faith. We were beginning a whole new lifestyle based on thinking positive, being creative and realizing the universe would serve up whatever we wanted if we just asked for it. We were both utilizing a personal philosophy of life taught at PSI World Seminars. PSI stands for People Synergistically Involved. Synergy is a combination of synchronicity and energy. It stands to reason that if your mind and body are "in sync," then energy will flow, positive energy that allows you to lead a creative and fulfilling life. When you are in total harmony with a loved one, life becomes blissful and exciting. That's what we were experiencing as we embarked on our trip to Florida.

PSI World was the brainchild of the late Thomas B. Wilhite who fervently believed that 'to think is to create.' Everything in the universe began with a thought including you and me. PSI World Seminars are designed to bring out the best in the individual as they discover their own strengths and weaknesses and things that may have been holding them back in their lives. Joanne's personal philosophies were in line with what PSI World was teaching. I started to write "preaching." Then, I realized that the mentors at PSI World weren't preaching. They were endowing us with tools to utilize every day. One of the biggest hurdles for more than a few people was being on time. Instructors let us know that we had a certain amount of time to get inside the classroom before the doors were closed. If a person came in after the doors were closed, they would be asked if that's how they live their lives, being late. Often, a person would feel insulted or feel they were being singled out and they would just leave rather than admit they were less than perfect.

Joanne's personal philosophies concurred with PSI World. There are no accidents." Everything happens for a reason. "There are no coincidences." That was difficult for me at first. I had to throw away most of my old worn out ways of thinking and open my mind to the possibilities. When the student is ready, the teacher will appear. I was almost ready. Joanne disdained the use of the word 'problems' and replaced it with 'challenges.' She believed in taking total responsibility for everything in our lives because we were the sum total of every event that had occurred up to that point, every road taken, every bridge crossed. "There are no victims, only volunteers." We could choose to be a victim or we could accept responsibility for our actions and learn from them. It was beginning to make sense to me. I was ready for the teachers to take me to a higher level of thinking.

Nothing illustrated my new way of thinking more than a little incident that occurred with the Hewlett-Packard bowling team. We bowled once a week and one week I informed my co-workers that I felt I was going to bowl a 200 game that night. I could already see the numbers up on the scoreboard above the lanes. I was using a PSI World tool called "Screen of The Mind." The results were awesome and that night when I bowled 220, I was blown out of the water.

There is a book called "Think And Grow Rich," by the late Napoleon Hill. One of the statements from that marvelous book is "Whatever the mind of man can conceive and believe, he can achieve." If you can visualize something before it happens, the chances are excellent that it will happen as you see it in your mind. First, you need to have a "burning desire." I had a burning desire to go east and get associated with the Boston Red Sox and I was making it happen with Joanne.

I had never heard of PSI World until Joanne introduced me to a PSI World guest event on our first date. I put up a lot of resistance at first. Resistance is the first of the "three R's," something else I learned in PSI World. Second is "Resentment" and third is "Revenge." I didn't resent learning something new. It was just that I felt after twenty years in the military a divorce from my first wife and the death of my second wife that I didn't feel I needed anyone or any organization to help me live my life. A nice glass of wine and a cigarette would take care of any problems, I mean, challenges.

In October, 1987, my second wife, Christine, passed away at the age of 45 due to complications from Primary Pulmonary Hypertension, an insidious illness with no cause and no cure. The greatest minds in medicine could not come to grips with an illness that seemed to strike predominantly women in their mid to late thirties. The blood flowing from the lungs to the heart was constricted forcing the heart to work extra hard to try and pump blood that just wasn't there. Nobody had an answer as to what causes the millions of blood vessels in the lungs to be constricted. The disease was complicated by the effects of high altitude, causing additional pressure on the heart muscle. A doctor once told me that Christine's condition was comparable to riding a bicycle uphill all the time. The heart continues to enlarge until it ultimately gives out.

The first signs of her illness were several fainting episodes that were scary and prompted us to go to the US Air Force Academy Hospital emergency room where she was diagnosed. The doctor explained as gently as possible that this was an incurable illness and patients generally survived for five to seven years. The next step was a heart catherization at Fitzsimmons Army Hospital in Denver. We were told that it would be highly advisable to move to a lower altitude. Christine had family members in northern California. I applied for a hardship transfer with Hewlett-Packard and we went to Roseville, California so Chris could breathe easier. For the next six years, she fought a courageous battle. She was in and out of hospitals until the last stop, a nursing home near Santa Rosa, California where this very brave young lady decided to stop taking her medications on the advice of her physician, Dr, Greg Hopkins, an eminent cardiologist and a man of great compassion. Chris had asked him how to end the suffering. On October 26th, 1987, she found peace. I was crushed. I had visited her that morning, then returned to work at HP in Rohnert Park, California, believing I would see her later that evening. I walked into the rest home around 5:30pm in the afternoon where a nurse met me in the hallway. She said, "Oh, Mr. Barney. Didn't they tell you?"

"Tell me what," I answered.

"Mrs. Barney expired."

Somehow, through my tears, I called family members around the country, then drove to Sacramento and picked up my step- daughter, Kim, who was enrolled at UC Davis. Kim was such a big help to me. We lived in a rented house in Tomales, California and Kim just took over, answering calls and making all the arrangements that had to be made for her mother at a Santa Rosa funeral home. Kim and I and

Christine's son, Kevin, made arrangements to have their mother's ashes scattered over redwood trees just east of the Little River Airport in Mendocino County. Incredibly, Joanne and I would later purchase property in 1996 very close to where the ashes probably landed. Christine's spirit was everywhere. Nothing illustrates this better than the song, *I Can See Clearly Now*. That was playing on the jukebox at the nightclub in Rapid City, South Dakota, where I met Christine. We decided that that was "our song." The year was 1972. I cannot tell you how many times Joanne and I have heard that song being played on the radio or over a supermarket music system in the past 23 years since Christine's passing. Do we all have angels or spirit guides watching over us all the time? Joanne and I like to think so.

    I coped with my grief by traveling to Massachusetts to visit my mother. My sister, Mary Frances and her husband, Jan Hatch, lived in Athol and I spent time with them as well as my brother, Bob, and his wife, Anne. It felt good to be around family for the holidays. I returned to my two bedroom Santa Rosa apartment in January, 1988.

    One Saturday night, I was at home, relaxing in my recliner, just kicked back and listening to my favorite radio station, KOIT in San Francisco. I was enjoying a glass of chilled white zinfandel and smoking a cigarette when I realized that my life was not going to change unless I took some action to make a change. I showered and shaved then drove to a nearby restaurant where I enjoyed a prime rib dinner and later, some good conversation with some people who were employed with me at HP in nearby Rohnert Park.

    I first went to work for Hewlett-Packard in Colorado Springs in 1979. I hand wrote my work resume' on yellow legal paper. When I was called in for an interview a couple of weeks later, I learned there were 100 applicants for the tech position I was seeking. My future boss, Mr. Bill Wessells, told me all the applications were on white paper except mine. Bill decided to read mine first. He liked it and he enjoyed the one-on-one interview. As I recall, we talked quite a bit about our mutual love, the Denver Broncos football team. There were a few technical questions that I handled easily. After working for Litton Industries, I was going to work for the best company in the United

States. There were no layoffs at HP and no time clocks. Everyone was on the honor system. "Flextime" allowed employees to come to work anytime between 6 and 8:30am, put in their eight hours and go home. The system worked well as did the coffee breaks with free donuts. Every Friday was "Aloha" Friday when employees would wear their Hawaiian shirts. We had profit sharing where the company matched every dollar that we put into our account. Every six months, the company would announce a profit sharing percentage which generally amounted to two weeks pay. Everyone at HP was addressed by their first name, even Dave Packard, one of the co-founders of the firm. On a visit to our facility, he let the employees know he wanted to be addressed by his first name. Nobody wore neckties and offices were all located in open cubicles. I remember having a beautiful view of Pike's Peak from my work station. Production goals were consistently met or exceeded and employee morale was always at a high level. We enjoyed some awesome month-ending beer parties when we hit our shipping targets for the Hewlett-Packard oscilloscopes. In short, it was an awesome place to work. When I was granted a hardship transfer to California, I was given a $250 a month pay increase. I had tears in my eyes at a going- away party in my honor.

After the delicious dinner, I drove to a place called Quincy's Pub in Rohnert Park where there was a live band and a lot of people. I sat at the end of a crowded bar, consumed a couple of glasses of wine then a little after midnight, I decided to return to my Santa Rosa apartment.

As I stepped outside, a girl said; "Smile, everyone in there is so serious." I smiled at her and we started talking. In a couple of minutes, we were joined by a gorgeous young redhead with a nice smile and a twinkle in her eyes. Her name was Roberta and her friend was Kathy who was very friendly, albeit a little goofy. Roberta asked me how old I was. I was a little surprised at the question but answered I was fifty. She told me her mom was a young fifty and the owner of the Human Touch School of Therapeutic Massage and healing Arts in Rohnert Park. That got my attention. Roberta was very attractive and I imagined that her mom must be attractive as well. When Roberta asked me if I would like to have her mom's phone number, my answer was an enthusiastic "yes." I didn't know it then but my earthly existence was about to undergo a radical transformation. I lingered at the pub for a while longer, even dancing with Kathy and betting with her on the outcome of the upcoming Super Bowl due to be played the next day between the Washington Redskins and Denver Broncos. The wager was a bottle of Jack Daniels. I would be rooting for the Broncos. When I left Quincy's at nearly 1 AM, I was a very happy man.

In the meantime, as I found out later, Roberta returned home to her mom's condo and told her she had met a man who would be calling her soon. Joanne had asked her daughter to be on the lookout for someone she might be interested in. Roberta told her that she met a man from Vermont named Elmer who was fifty and was also a smoker. That didn't set well with Joanne who had no desire to date a smoker. Nonetheless, she looked forward to my call.

I had no prior knowledge of this exchange between mother and daughter when I called the next day and learned that Joanne was visiting her daughter in Petaluma. I decided I would call her the next night. It turned out to be a lousy Sunday. Denver got their butts kicked by the Redskins but I had something to look forward to on Monday.

The next evening, Joanne and I talked for more than two hours and arranged to meet at the Flamingo Hotel and restaurant the following Wednesday night. My Chinese Pug, Pepper Puss, was in my lap while I chatted with Joanne and at one point, I asked her if she wanted to hear a pug snort. That broke her up and she realized that I loved animals. She also loved the sound of my voice and she was looking forward to meeting me. When I went to work the next day, I was walking on air. I had a date.

Wednesday evening, I was waiting for Joanne in the lounge of the Flamingo Hotel in Santa Rosa. Around 5:30 PM, she came inside, wearing a long aqua skirt with a matching long shirt. She looked very nice and I knew in my heart that she was indeed "the one." We had a drink and got acquainted, then it was time to go into the room where the PSI World guest event was being held. It was graduates of PSI Basic, a three day introductory seminar. Every one of them was jazzed as they told the audience about the positive effect PSI World was already having on their lives. It was an enjoyable evening but I wasn't sold on PSI World until Joanne took me out to dinner on my 51st birthday and explained some of the positive thinking concepts to me over drinks and a prime rib dinner at the same Santa Rosa restaurant I had gone to before going to Quincy's Pub. Joanne spent $100 that night and I was impressed. It was a very nice birthday gift. She had a PhD in Education and Counseling and she was working very hard at teaching students how to become therapeutic massage experts. Joanne was renting space in a building in Rohnert Park where she was the sole proprietor of The Human Touch School of Therapeutic Massage and Healing Arts. She was charging her students $800 for several weeks of instruction that would lead to a diploma and certification as a legitimate massage therapist. The school was approved by the State of California which was a good thing.

The school was not making very much money which wasn't such a good thing. The bigger picture, a lifelong relationship with a beautiful very youthful looking lady, looked pretty good to me especially after being the recipient of several full body massages.

Our next date was a movie called *Good Morning, Vietnam*, starring Robin Williams. Afterward, we returned to my apartment for wine and conversation. One thing led to another and Joanne called her daughter to let her know she wouldn't be home that night. Our lovemaking was beautiful as if we were made for each other, as if we were meant to spend the rest of our lives together. I kept making comments like "and when we're married," much to Joanne's consternation. She had been through several relationships and had given birth to three beautiful daughters in the process. Any talk of marriage set off an alarm. At one point, it triggered an attack of "hives." Don't say the "m" word, she said to me more than once.

Our third date was an evening in Joanne's hot tub on the patio of her condo. As we relaxed and drank wine, Joanne let me know she had visualized a man with gray eyebrows using "screen of the mind," sitting across from her in the hot tub. It was a very romantic evening made more so when Joanne sang *You Light Up My Life*, just for me.

Roberta was engaged to Dave, a career Coast Guard man who was stationed at Two Rock Coast Guard Base, a few miles west of Petaluma. Roberta was the mother of two children from a previous marriage, two boys named Jeremy and Joshua. She and Dave were contemplating their wedding date.

Meanwhile, Joanne suggested that I could go to work for the Human Touch and help promote her business. I thought that was a pretty good idea, so I gave a two week notice to Hewlett-Packard, collected $7,000 in severance pay and bought Joanne a diamond ring. We flew back to the East coast so Joanne could meet my mother and gain her approval of my wife-to-be. While we were in Massachusetts, we went out for a lobster dinner. My mother watched Joanne devour a two pound lobster at one sitting and thought she was a very cool lady. It would be the last time I would see my mother. She passed away in October, 1989 at the age of 75.

Joanne and Roberta put their heads together and started making plans for a most unique double wedding ceremony on a boat at beautiful Lake Tahoe, California. Somehow, it all came together. We drove to Lake Tahoe on the 1st of July, 1988, and after a night of partying and some gambling, everyone boarded the boat on July 2nd. Lori, Joanne's oldest daughter, was there with her husband, Chris and daughter, Julia. Marlene was there with her husband, Leo, and their son, Evan. Marlene was pregnant, about two weeks away from arrival of her second child, a truly amazing event since she was wheelchair bound as the result of a motorcycle accident in 1982. Samantha Ella Hatch was born on July 16th. Right now, in July, 2010, Sammy has graduated from Columbia School of Drama in Chicago and is looking forward to a career in the entertainment business. We are very proud of her. Two of our other grandchildren, Jeremy and Joshua, are both married and fathers of our great grandsons, Eli, who was born to Joshua and Alyson on May 3rd, 2009. Meanwhile, our second great grandson, Xavier was born on April 28th, 2010. Dad Jeremy is in the U.S. Navy. He and his wife, Mary are currently in Germany.

The Tahoe weather was sunny and beautiful as the captain steered the boat to a nearby cove where the water was calm. We had a Kenny

Rogers CD playing *Lady.* Joanne and I considered that to be our song. On the inside of my wedding ring, Joanne had these words inscribed: '"I'm your lady." The captain, who was slightly inebriated, prepared to perform the ceremony. Dave and Roberta and Joanne and I stood in front of him as he read the wedding vows, then said; "Roberta, do you take Elmer?" Roberta quickly corrected him and the rest of the double wedding ceremony went on with no further miscues. Afterward, we all drank champagne. Evan and Julia both had an opportunity to steer the boat and we all had a good time. The four of us went to Hawaii for a honeymoon after catching a "hop" from Travis Air Force Base, California. Flying free with the Air Force is a wonderful benefit that both active duty and retired members enjoy. My dear friends, Bill and Mary Geiser, had access to a condo in Waipahu on the island of Oahu. Bill's son met us at Hickam Air Force Base and gave us the keys while he went off to the mainland. The four of us enjoyed an absolutely delightful ten days, much of it spent on the beautiful beaches of the Aloha State. Bill's son graciously allowed us to use his car and we drove around the island more than once.

Joanne and I returned to a rented house in Newark, California, near Fremont where she was running the second Human Touch School. A PSI World classmate of Joanne told her of the vacant building in Fremont where she could open her school. He said he would help her out financially. Joanne and I attempted to sell "on site" massage to both small and large businesses but we were about ten years ahead of ourselves as the business community and many individuals still looked on massage as an unlawful activity. My, how the times have changed in a couple of decades.

We went to dinner with a wealthy PSI World graduate, a delightful man named Jack. He was willing to put up $20,000 in stocks to bankroll the Human Touch. Meanwhile, I had already graduated from PSI Basic and enrolled in PSI Five, a five day course designed to empower everyone into believing that they can be successful in all they strive to create. Sadly, the money that Jack put up wasn't enough to save the Fremont school. It didn't help that Joanne's "friend," Timothy, backed down on his offer to help her pay the rent every month which was over $2,000 a month. Timothy had no intention of helping Joanne. Everything closed in Fremont and we went back to Rohnert Park. We were living in Joanne's fifth wheel and contemplating our future by March, 1989. In El Cajon, California, Roberta gave birth to a daughter, Jenna, conceived in Hawaii. Joanne sold the Human Touch School to a man who ultimately ripped her off and stole the business from her. He gave her a Shell credit card to use and we decided to take the fifth wheel across the USA to my 35th high school class reunion at Danville High School in Danville, Vermont. I was excited to be back in my home state.

I was born at Brightlook Hospital in Saint Johnsbury, Vermont, on February 17th, 1937. After spending the first five years of my life in St. Johnsbury, our family, which included my younger brother Bob and a baby sister, Mary Frances, moved to East Boston, Massachusetts where our father, Elmer, worked for the United States Army as a civilian weapons inspector. I was too young to know what was going on in the world but I do recall that our parents had to pull the window shades down at night in the east Boston housing project we lived in. That was a precaution against any air attacks the enemy forces might attempt to carry out.

My dad enjoyed taking me to games at Fenway Park when I was eight years old. I remember the streetcars and the subway rides and the ten cent ferry boat ride across the harbor to Boston. Dad was born and raised in Orange, Massachusetts and he had been following the Red Sox since the nineteen twenties. The walk from the subway station at Kenmore Square was exciting because there were always a lot of fans and everyone was talking about the Red Sox. On the left side of the street, before walking across the bridge over what is now the Mass. Turnpike, there was a White Tower hamburger restaurant and my dad would always be ready to buy a couple of burgers which were probably selling for fifty cents. Tickets for the grandstand were only a couple of dollars. I don't recall much about 1945 but 1946 was when my awareness of the Red Sox soared. I had black and white photos of every member of the team and it was so exciting when they got to the World Series, even though they lost. They never lost my support.

When Joanne and I returned from the cross country trip to Vermont, we took the fifth wheel to the incredibly beautiful Mendocino coast of northern California where we would both work as massage therapists in a rustic little settlement called Caspar, located halfway between Ft. Bragg and the lovely town of Mendocino. We parked the fifth wheel in a rented space at Caspar Beach campground, across the road from a nice beach and the awesome night sound of the roaring surf. Joanne and I both worked at a beautiful place called The Mendocino Tubs, a very popular weekend destination for both locals and people coming up from the San Francisco bay area. The tubs offered full body massages and hour or longer soaks in the awesome redwood hot tubs that we used every night when we finished giving massages to other people. Our cat, Caspar, loved it. He would run and play and nip at the heels of unsuspecting victims. He loved nothing better than going up on to the roof of a dressing room and forcing me to rescue him even though he could have come down by himself. There was nothing quite as delicious as soaking in a 104 degree redwood hot tub with the jets running and Joanne and I gazing at the stars.

I loved the Mendocino coast. It was home to many artists, authors, musicians and poets and vagabonds like ourselves. I had fallen in love with the coast before meeting Joanne when I used to drive Christine to Mendocino where she could breathe the moist sea air. She loved the coast. Ultimately, we would sell our home in Rocklin, California and relocate to a rented house in Ft. Bragg where I would drive two and a half hours one way on the ever-dangerous Highway 128, to go to work for HP in Rohnert Park. I would arrive home at seven o'clock at night, have dinner, then rise at 4am the next morning and do the same thing all over again. It only lasted for a month. The stress was taking its toll on me. I decided we had to move closer to my work but still be fairly close to the ocean. Chris was brokenhearted at leaving the Mendocino coast. It was a gut wrenching decision. We chose the little town of Tomales where I cannot say enough good things about the kind and gentle inhabitants. Chris was very sick by then and bedridden most of the time. People would bring hot meals to the house. Total strangers called to ask how they could help. A local church raised money to help me pay more than $3,000 in medical bills. To this day, I am deeply indebted to those wonderful people who cared so much about us.

Two

When I met Joanne, I also met Bonnie, her beautiful Irish Setter. Bonnie loved to ride in the Dodge Colt, taking up most of the back seat. She would sleep most of the way from Santa Rosa to the school in Fremont. She would start getting very excited when we arrived in Fremont where there was a large open field with lots of bushes, trees and shrubs and rodents. Bonnie would run and look for ground squirrels and anything else that piqued her interest. As we neared the field, she would stick her head out the window and start shaking in anticipation of being let out of the car. As soon as the door opened, she was off and running, often stopping and pointing her tail in a classic Irish Setter pose. She was so beautiful. I enjoyed letting her take me for walks. When we moved up to the coast, Bonnie was delighted. There was lots of room on the bluffs for her to run and play. One day, I became alarmed when she just fell while she was running. I had to carry her back to the car, then take her to the vet. Bonnie had an incurable illness, a form of doggie leukemia that was destroying her red blood cells. Her running days were over. We watched, helplessly as she grew weaker and weaker. Joanne held her beautiful head in her lap and kept her warm. It was so hard to understand why our beloved dog's life was ebbing away. Ultimately, we had her euthanized and buried her near a cemetery overlooking the ocean so her spirit was free. She would run and play in animal heaven forever. We cried a lot.

Shortly after Bonnie's death in October, 1989, Joanne received news that her friend of many years was dying at Letterman Army Hospital in San Francisco. She rushed to his bedside, arriving in time to be with him the last few minutes of his life. Almost simultaneously, we received word that Joanne's stepfather had passed away in Petaluma and two days later, I was notified that my mother had passed away in Massachusetts. I was driving toward Travis AFB, California to get a flight with the Air Force. I had just arrived in Vacaville, California and I was listening to the World Series game being played in San Francisco when a mammoth earthquake rumbled through the Bay Area, collapsing highways, starting fires in San Francisco and stopping the baseball game being played at Candlestick Park. It was as if the universe was challenging both of us to cope with life and death. There was so much to be learned about both subjects and we didn't know it but the challenges were just beginning

When Joanne and I moved to Mendocino County, I let her know that I wanted to be "in the air," and "on the air." I had a burning desire to be in radio broadcasting, an ambition I had coveted since graduation from Danville High in 1954. Twenty years in the Air Force came first.

Near the end of my Air Force career, I was stationed at Ellsworth AFB, South Dakota, in the beautiful Black Hills. I met and became friends with Jim Shaw, the program director for KIMM, a local AM station. One night, over drinks, in the local Holiday Inn, I convinced him I should be on the radio. I will never forget my first day on the air, at 6 am on a Sunday morning. We were using 45 rpm records and big turntables. Somehow, I flipped the wrong switch and put the station off the air. I had to call Jim at 6:30 to tell him two turntables were not working. He had never heard of a situation like that. He got me squared away. I got the station back on the air and I was okay after that. Years later, we laughed about it. "Captain Jimmy," as he was known to Rapid City listeners, went on to become the mayor of Rapid City, South Dakota. We had some good times together.

By 1990, I was working at KSAY in Fort Bragg and interviewing many

Boston sports personalities as part of my newscasts. My motto was, "We don't just read the news. We put people in it." In my spare time, I wrote about the Red Sox. That's when Joanne suggested we go to Florida. Prior to the KSAY job, I was employed at KDAC, an old AM station in Ft. Bragg. One morning, I was hosting a program called "Swap Shop," where people called in with items for sale or to give away. A lady called and said she had newborn kittens to give away. Joanne was listening and heard her birth date in the phone number. She considered that to be an omen. She went to the house and looked at the kittens that were in a cardboard box. One of them was a male Lynx-point Siamese who came right to Joanne. She cradled him in her arms and later brought him to the radio station so I could see him. He was beautiful. We named him Caspar, after the little town where we lived and worked. In 1995, a lady named Joanne Fisher wrote an article about us and our cat and it was published in the Mendocino Beacon under Village Vignettes. The article follows:

> He has over 36,000 miles on him. He's been up and down the coast from Oregon to San Diego and back and forth across the United States three times.
>
> Does that sound like a classified ad you might find in the auto-motive column? Try the animals section.
>
> This traveling man is a 16 pound Lynx Point Siamese who goes by the name of Caspar. When he's not at home, he tours in grand style in a motor home with his devoted owners of five years, Caspar residents Joanne and Barney.
>
> If Caspar crossed your path, you'd be tempted to call Fish and Game. This guy is three feet long. One whole yardstick, from the tip of his pink nose to the tip of his hind paw. His long tail is marked like a raccoon, and his face looks like the lynx you've probably seen in National Geographic.
>
> Before their marriage seven years ago, Joanne had an Irish Setter who had seen her through some pretty

rough times, including an accident that left one of her three daughters a paraplegic.

When her dog died of leukemia, she says, "I had such a big empty pot in my heart. I just had to fill it up."

She was listening to the Swap Shop on the radio and heard about a litter of kittens. The number to call contained all the numbers of her birthday. She knew in her heart one of those kittens was going to be hers.

They had no idea he was destined to take up so much room, in their home, in their camper, and in their hearts.

Joanne, a retired school teacher, was living with her daughter when Barney came into her life. She'd asked her daughter, Roberta, to keep an eye open for a "decent guy."

After an evening out, Roberta said, "Mom, some guy's going to be calling you. His name is Barney. Really, his name is Elmer, but he goes by Barney."

Barney's forgiven Joanne for her response. "Oh wow, that sounds like Clem Kadiddlehopper!" She says when Barney called, "His voice did it for me. We talked for over two hours. I fell for the voice before I met the guy."

Joanne also says, "I'm into meditation, visualization and affirmation. I visualized the man of my dreams as having grey eyebrows. When I finally met Barney, I said, 'Oh my god! I conjured him up.'"

After they got together, they used to ask each other, "Are we having fun yet?" At the time, Joanne was teaching healing arts in Oakland. She says, "Here I was teaching stress reduction and breaking out in hives!" That realization culminated in their move to the coast.

It's not surprising to find out that Barney's voice

opened the door to Joanne's heart and to a childhood dream. "I've had a love affair with radio since I was six years old," Barney says.

When he told Joanne that he'd always dreamed of being "on the air and in the air," they visualized Barney's dream. He created a job for himself.

With a natural voice for radio, Barney not only fulfilled a childhood dream, but a high school yearbook prediction as well. He is the other half of Fred and Barney, also known as "Flyin High with the Good News Guys," broadcasting on KSAY weekdays from 8 to 9am. His favorite phrase is "Livin' and lovin' on the shores of the Mendocino coast." And he's taking flying lessons.

The Barneys have had to track Caspar down more than a few times during their travels. Once he got lost in the corn fields of Illinois and once they bought about 50 dollars worth of pizza and ice cream for a bunch of kids who found Caspar after a five day search.

Barney, Joanne and Caspar are inseparable. When Barney gets his pilot's license, Caspar the flying cat is going to have to learn fast that his litter box is back on Terra Firma.

We had a Ford pickup truck and Joanne would drive ten miles to KDAC to pick me up at night after I signed off the air. While waiting outside, she taught our very intelligent cat to play baseball. I should say that he taught her. She would use a stick to bat little round acorns or stones and Caspar would catch the objects then run around the bases she placed on the ground. It was as if he knew that he was going to be involved with baseball. It was as if this sweet little bundle of fur knew exactly why he was part of our family. Our great adventure together would begin soon.

After saying goodbye to Joanne's daughters Marlene and Roberta and their families, Joanne and I and Caspar departed from Petaluma in our Dodge Colt, bound for Winter Haven, Florida and Red Sox spring training. The car was filled with our personal possessions, the big word processor, a big video camera, Caspar's litter box, a couple of suitcases and Caspar. Just south of Bakersfield on Interstate 5 is a stretch of highway called the "Grapevine." We encountered heavy snow as we climbed toward the summit. I remember hearing Caspar emit some nervous meows as we followed a snowplow in "Southern California." The snow quickly melted as we descended into the San Fernando Valley after which we would head east toward Phoenix on Interstate 10. Our intent was to stop to visit my Aunt Julia and her son, Mike, in Chandler, Arizona. We stayed overnight in the modest little home on West Laredo Drive, then headed toward El Paso, Texas the next day.

Aunt Julia was a sweet lady. She always served up some of her fantastic peach cobbler while my cousin and I would talk sports for hours. Mike seemed to know every player on every team in baseball, basketball and football. Additionally, he had statistics on all the players and this was long before personal computers were all the rage. The people in Chandler loved Mike. He was the chemistry teacher at Chandler High School and he was also known as "Coach Barney" for his involvement in school sports. Mike never married. He was content to live with his mother for many years after his father passed away. Mike loved to drive his Datsun 280Z, loved growing several varieties of roses and loved eating enormous amounts of food. That would eventually be his undoing. He developed diabetes and kidney disease. By 2006 when Joanne and I went to see him, his condition was worsening. Aunt Julia had passed away in 2002 and Mike just didn't take very good care of himself after that. In late January, 2007, Mike went to the hospital with chest pains and other complications. He fully expected to recover and come home, telling friends and siblings he was going to give roses to all the nurses for their great care. Sadly, Mike passed away on the morning of February 2nd, 2007. We had talked about the Red Sox on the phone the night before he died. He was reading the sports page and joking with his nurses when his heart stopped functioning. If he had to choose a way to leave reading the sports page would have been exactly what he wanted to be doing. Mike was 58 years old. He and I enjoyed watching a lot of football during the holidays in 2006. I felt so good that I was there for him, not knowing it was the last few weeks of his life. Just a few days after Christmas, Joanne and I and Mike went to a movie called "We Are Marshall." It was the last movie Mike ever attended. Of course, it was about football. Rest in peace, cousin Mike.

Another first cousin on my father's side of the family was former Vermont Chief Justice Albert W. Barney Jr. of St. Johnsbury. Over the years, I visited Judge Barney every time I was in Vermont. He loved the Red Sox and I enjoyed talking baseball and other things with him. I always told friends and relatives that "Al" had knowledge of everything there was to know about in the world. In 1946, he helped my father get settled into our new home in North Danville. Judge Barney was twenty-five years old and had just finished a tour of duty with the U.S. Navy. This was after four years at Yale, then two years of post-graduate work at Harvard Law School. He was on the Dean's List every year. In 1953, during his early years as a Caledonia County Judge, he hired me to work at his ice cream stand in St. Johnsbury. It was an unforgettable summer and gave me invaluable experience for the real world of going to work for a living.

I enlisted in the Air Force in 1954 and served for twenty years, retiring in 1974 at the age of 37 with an honorable discharge. I visited and spoke with Judge Barney and his wife, Helen, many times from 1974 to 2007 when I organized a family reunion while a patient in the hospital in Scottsdale, Arizona. There had not been a Barney family reunion for more than thirty years and I knew time was running out for a last chance for the Barney clan to get together in one place. We decided to have it at a restaurant in St. Johnsbury. Judge Barney, who was 86 by then, would only be required to travel a short distance from his home to the restaurant. My brother, Bob, came up with his wife, Anne, from Massachusetts. My sister Mary Frances and her husband Jan drove me up from Athol, Massachusetts, where I was visiting from my home in Colorado. My cousin John Barney, a retired USAF

Lieutenant Colonel, was present with his wife, Brenda. Cousin Kathy, Mike's sister, came in from Arizona with her daughter. Of course, the guest of honor was the Honorable Judge and his lovely wife, Helen, with two of their three daughters, Marianne and Kathy. Everyone enjoyed the day, especially Judge Barney who loved telling stories about our ancestors.

Judge Barney was forced to be in his house most of the time after that year. Joanne and I visited him in March, 2010. Though feeling very sick, his mind was sharp as he recalled some good times over the years. He passed away on May 10th, at his home in St. Johnsbury. He was a great and compassionate judge with an equally great intellect. He will be missed. May he rest in peace.

THREE

When Joanne and I stopped at a small motel on the eastern end of El Paso, Texas, we got the word processor out of the car and wrote a couple of pages. We decided to call our story "Love Those Red Sox." because so many people rooted for them and they had been my very favorite team since my boyhood. All that has changed. It's 2010 and after reading an earlier version of the manuscript, my brother-in-law and acting editor, Jan Hatch, said, "your book is more about you than it is about the Red Sox." Jan hit the proverbial nail on the head and I took a totally different approach to the story by adding "One Man's Baseball Journey," to the original title. It has been and continues to be a journey of life and loving the fact that we are putting the finishing touches on a story we hope will have some mass appeal.

We arrived in Winter Haven and checked into an inexpensive motel. I felt so excited. It was hard to sleep that night because I was anticipating going to the ballpark and seeing the Red Sox in spring training.

We went to Chain-O-Lakes Stadium the following morning, found a parking space, then made our way to the office where Josh Spofford of the Red Sox public relations department introduced himself and gave us credentials for the parking lot and the ballpark area.

As we were standing there, Johnny Pesky walked in. He looked tanned and fit. "Wow," I said to him. "Forty-five years ago, I was watching you play at Fenway Park. Now, we're meeting face to face and I feel as if I've known you all my life." I introduced Joanne, then we went into the office area where we encountered Lou Gorman, the general manager of the team. Joanne explained to Lou that we were writing a positive story about the team and that it would be up to them to be positive all season. Lou agreed, smiled and said they would be positive all year. We were already having a good effect on the team.

I felt like a kid in a candy store as Joanne and I walked around the spring training complex. I recognized Dan Shaughnessy, the curly-haired Irishman from the Boston Globe and the author of "The Curse of The Bambino." We had Dan's book with us and he signed it for us after we told him about our book.

Red Sox right fielder Tom Brunansky was sitting outside the clubhouse taking a break. I approached him with Joanne by my side, introduced ourselves and asked Tom for an interview. He smiled and said it was okay. He was very cordial as I asked him about his career and his thoughts on positive thinking. "Bruno," as he was known to his teammates, gave us some wonderful insights into the life of a big league ballplayer.

"Everybody has their own story of how they got here. To me, number one is the love of the game. There's so much time and so many hours spent with countless practices and Little League games, then high school and way up the line. You certainly have to have the support of parents to take you to practices and get you signed up, get you involved. There are so many things and so many people behind the scenes. I'm one of the fortunate few to get a professional contract and have a chance to play every day in the major leagues. It's the dream of every youngster to play on a World Championship club. I've experienced that and I can tell you it's a tremendous feeling." Tom was referring to his playing for the Minnesota Twins when they defeated the St. Louis Cardinals and won the 1987 World Series. He commented on our book. "On the focus of your book, I feel we have a pretty good chance of winning it all this year. I heard Peter Gammons say on ESPN that with all the talent we have here, we stand a pretty good chance of winning it all. But, if we didn't, hell hath no fury like a scorned Red Sox fan." We laughed at Tom's remark.

I explained that Joanne was a retired schoolteacher and not much of a baseball fan. She thought the World Series was always between the Yankees and the Dodgers. Joanne told Tom she sometimes gets the Super Bowl and the World Series mixed up. He made sure Joanne understood the difference by telling her to remember that in baseball, it's runs and not points.

Tom wrapped up our interview by discussing the clubhouse atmosphere. And he talked about leadership qualities. "Baseball has changed so much. What we really need is the quiet leadership, you know, guys that just go out and have fun. There is so much pressure put on the players, from the media, from yourselves, from the fans, the money that's out there. There are so many distractions from the game that take away from the whole aspect of it and like I say, that's to go out and have fun. You try and keep it as plain and simple as you can, but it will put you in perspective real easy."

I asked Tom about his family.

"I've been married for five years, have a little boy, Jason, who's 16months and another on the way, due in September. There you go. Hopefully, it will be a good year all around."

We thanked Tom for his time as he headed off toward the clubhouse. My first interview with a big league ballplayer was a success. A few years later in my radio broadcasting career, I would often feature telephone interviews with Tom from his home in the San Diego area. He never turned down a request to be on my program. He was always candid and gracious as we enjoyed some great conversations. And Tom Brunansky remains a good friend to this day. He is a class act.

Our second full day at spring training was rainy and cool. Joanne took the car and went off to look for a place to live while I hung out in the press room and listened to Boston area newspaper reporters telling stories and kibitzing about Red Sox players. It was fascinating stuff for a neophyte like myself. At one point, I turned on my noisy word processor just as a reporter from the Herald was calling in a story. I was admonished the next day by Jim Samia, a rather hard-nosed public relations guy for the Red Sox. From that point on, I kept the word processor off.

Joanne returned later in the day with good news. She had located a place to live. It turned out to be a huge old trailer home that rented by the week at a rate that fit into our spartan budget. There was ample space, a huge living room with a sofa and a couple of easy chairs, a large kitchen area and two bedrooms. Caspar made himself right at home, getting friendly with a family of Possum that lived under the flooring and had a hole in the floor in the walk-in closet in our bedroom. They didn't bother us and we didn't bother them. We just co-existed peacefully. We were comfortable in Florida but not for long. When the Red Sox went up north to Boston, our intent was to go with them.

The lunch room at the ballpark was the focal point for meeting people that were associated with baseball in some capacity. I looked forward to lunch breaks because I never knew who would be in line with me as Wanda and George served up the fries and burgers. Johnny Pesky was beside me one day and we were talking baseball. Somehow, the conversation drifted around to 1946 and Johnny bristled. "Are you going to bring that up again, Barney?" he said, referring to the infamous incident in the 1946 World Series when Enos Slaughter of the St. Louis cardinals scored the winning run. Johnny quickly let me know he was just kidding. I felt relieved.

A couple of days later just prior to the start of an exhibition game, I was pleasantly surprised to be in line with Brooks Robinson, the Hall of fame third baseman for the Baltimore Orioles for so many years. His fielding statistics were incredible and he was a great hitter as well. Brooks told me he was visiting Winter Haven as a representative of the Spalding Corporation. On another occasion, the Detroit Tigers were over from their spring home in nearby Lakeland. This time, the man behind me was Sparky Anderson, the former colorful manager of the "Big Red Machine," an affectionate term for the Cincinnati Reds. In 1991, Sparky was managing the Tigers. "I love Boston fans," he said. "Every year, they tell me the same thing: 'Wait till next year.'" It was a good-natured reference to the fact the Red Sox hadn't won a World Series since 1918.

One afternoon prior to an exhibition game with the Houston Astros, decided to sit at a table in the lunch room with a man who had an array of photography accessories and a sketchpad on the table. My first thought was that he must be the official photographer for the Red Sox. I sat down and introduced myself and learned that his name was George "Bud" Guzzi, a renowned artist whose works are on display at the Smithsonian Institution, the New England Sports Museum, NASA, the White House, many military installations and dozens of private collections. George has crafted paintings of movie stars Susan Sarandon and Sophia Loren, athletes Larry Bird and Bobby Orr, Mrs. Dennis Eckersley and many other prominent people in the world of sports and entertainment. In addition, he's the creator of the original Stat Trek poster with Captain Kirk, Spock, Scotty and the other colorful characters. He also creates acrylic landscapes that are incredibly detailed and beautiful.

A day after meeting George, I watched, fascinated as he created a pen and ink sketch of Harry Ellis Dickson, a jovial man who was then the associate conductor of the world famous Boston Pops Orchestra. Mr. Dickson was visiting Red Sox training camp and thoroughly enjoying the role of being a fan of the team

"I'll be the envy of all my colleagues back in Boston," he quipped.

As he sat quietly for the drawing, he said; "There are two jewels in the crown of the City of Boston, the Boston Pops and the Boston Red Sox." Mr. Dickson could conceivably have added the Boston Celtics and the Boston Bruins, the other two jewels. He was totally delighted with the finished sketch.

The Red Sox were enjoying a pretty good spring training. Roger, "the Rocket" Clemens was feeling good. A new addition to the club, slugger Jack Clark, was looking forward to hitting homers over the friendly left field wall at Fenway Park. Much was expected from two veteran outfielders, Mike Greenwell and Ellis Burks. The players were anxious to start the regular season. Optimism was high as the team prepared to break camp and travel north to Boston.

Hall of Famer Bobby Doerr's birthday was coming up on April 7th and I found the perfect card for him in a Lakeland supermarket, close to our rented home. I had a great time having the card signed by many players and Red Sox officials. Manager Joe Morgan was working with his outfielders when I asked him to sign the card.

"Betcha I can guess his age," Joe said. "He'll be 73." Joe was right on as he wrote, "Bobby, one of the best. Happy 73." Lou Gorman wrote, "Bobby, have a great birthday and many more to come. If anyone who ever played the game had more class than you, I've never met him. A true Hall of Famer and you represent the very best of baseball and the Red Sox." Hall of Famer Carl Yastrzemski signed his autograph along with Wade Boggs, Mike Greenwell and Ellis Burks.

It seemed as if we had just arrived in Winter Haven when all of a sudden it was time to load the Dodge Colt and head north. The two weeks spent with the Red Sox players were awesome. The interview with Tom Brunansky topped my highlight list. Getting to know Johnny Pesky was very special. Listening to his baseball stories at the end of each day made me realize why so many people liked him. He was always warmhearted and friendly and I really had the feeling that I had known him for many years. It was just the beginning of our relationship.

Joanne enjoyed meeting Johnny as well. She was so supportive, keeping me focused on the writing and making sure I didn't waste my time at the ballpark. We were both very excited at the prospect of going up to Boston and continuing our writing, not knowing what each day would bring in the way of surprises or challenges. We looked forward to visiting George and Rita Guzzi at their home in West Newton, a suburb of Boston. George had sketches of most of the players on the 1991 team and he offered to add some of his work to our book. Rita Guzzi teaches art in the basement of their home and her paintings of race horses are astounding. Joanne and I felt privileged to know both of these enormously talented artists.

Four

We arrived in the Boston area after the drive up from Florida. The little Dodge Colt was wonderful. We felt the change in the air temperature with the warmth of Florida replaced by the chill of New England in early spring. One of our first stops was at a McDonald's store in Dorchester, a Boston suburb where our attention was immediately drawn to a Ronald McDonald calendar. The month of April featured a crayola drawing of a girl in a Red Sox uniform. The caption beneath read: "I want to be the first girl pitcher on the Boston Red Sox." It was perfect for our story. "We must have this," I said to Joanne. She agreed and the store owner was happy to give us a calendar. The drawing was done by a girl named Jennifer Pava, age eleven. We would ultimately search for her without success. However, I did have the drawing signed by Ted Williams, Bobby Doerr, Johnny Pesky, Dom DiMaggio, Carl Yastrzemski, Luis Tiant and Reggie Jackson. I erred by not making a copy. Sadly, the document was stolen from my briefcase many years later by a man we had trusted as a caregiver. He turned out to be a two-bit thief and chiseler.

We managed to locate a basement studio apartment in Revere, at 69 Victoria Street, not far from East Boston where I had lived as a young boy from age five to nine. I remembered how my dad would take us out to Revere Beach when it had an amusement park and nightclubs. By the nineties, those amenities were long gone, replaced by high-rise apartment buildings. Revere was a good town, featuring some of the greatest pizza parlors on the east coast. I submit that there is nothing quite as delicious as an east coast pizza.

The apartment was adequate for our needs. The rent was inexpensive and it was only a short walk to the local Massachusetts Transit Authority (MTA) where I could catch the subway for the half hour ride to Kenmore Square and Fenway Park.

With the first challenge handled, the second challenge was to obtain credentials to cover the Red Sox at Fenway Park. I was so naive. I thought I could just walk in and inform them that I was a freelance writer. Surely, Dick Bresciani would recognize me from Winter Haven and grant instant approval. Joanne accompanied me to the Red Sox offices at 4 Yawkey Way. We encountered a chaotic scene. There were quite a few other people attempting to get press credentials besides myself. I wasn't the only person interested in covering the Red Sox. It was two days before the opening bell for the 1991 season. I asked Mr. Bresciani for credentials and he asked me if I had a publisher. "Everybody wants to write about the Red Sox," he said to me. I informed him I did not have a publisher, then I slunk away with my head down and my ego severely deflated. I felt crushed. As Joanne and I left the chaos of the PR office, we encountered Johnny Pesky, seated at a desk in a small cubicle. We told him what had just taken place. "For crissake, Barn, don't you have anyone in California that will back you up on this project? Have them send a fax to Bresciani."

Immediately, I thought of John Fremont and Cindy at Cypress House in Ft. Bragg, right next door to KSAY where I used to work. I sent a fax to John and like a pinch-hitter coming through in the bottom of the ninth with the bases loaded, John delivered for us. The next day, I reappeared at 4 Yawkey Way and received my press credentials from an amazed Dick Bresciani. The fax that John sent to the Red Sox requested that the Boston Red Sox extend all amenities to one 'Barney Deaton,' (my pen name at the time), as he collected material for *Love Those Red Sox*.

Oh happy days! I was in! I was in! The dreams I had harbored since age eleven, when I would gaze longingly up at the press box area and wish I could be up there, were coming true. Thanks to Johnny Pesky's suggestion, I had achieved my goal. I thanked God and I thanked John Fremont. I thanked Joanne for the love and support she was giving me.

I was given a large blue tag with "Opening Day" stamped on it. There was a string attached so I could wear it around my neck. The credentials allowed me access to the field. They did not include the press box or the clubhouse. Those privileges would come later in the season.

Joanne and I took the "T" the next day, from Revere to Kenmore Square, then we walked with throngs of people across the bridge over the Massachusetts Turnpike, then past the Cask & Flagon, a very popular watering hole on Lansdowne St., directly beneath the nets atop the left field wall. (All that has changed now. When the present owners took over, they made major improvements to Fenway Park, including putting seats atop the left field wall, called "Monster Seats." Fenway was already "the place to watch a game." Under the creative ownership of John Henry, Tom Werner and Larry Lucchino, the park became an extraordinary place to watch baseball, albeit very expensive for the average baseball fan.)

We had a pair of tickets for Section 20, behind home plate in an area reserved for guests of the Red Sox. The opening day opponent was the Cleveland Indians. I recall that the weather was not conducive to baseball. April in Boston usually means a cold north wind will be blowing. How many other guys, I wondered, would like to be doing what I was doing that day? Joanne located a seat. I kissed her, then armed with a notebook and a small Sony tape recorder, I made my way down toward the playing field where an usher opened a gate for me and said, "Welcome to opening day." I returned the smile and thanked him, then for the first time in my life, I stepped on to the green grass of Fenway Park. I must say a few words about the "old girl" here.

I refer to Fenway in the feminine gender because over the years, she has been like a woman, teasing and tantalizing, always looking gorgeous and ready for a nice evening but sometimes being very mischievous and mysterious. She gives and she takes. She can create jubilation or frustration, joy or heartbreak but she is always exciting and it was such an awesome privilege for me to experience her allure. My mind flashed back to Monday, October 3rd, 1948 when dad and I had seats in Section 20 to watch the first playoff game in the history of the American League. The opponent that day was also the Cleveland Indians, playing to see who would represent the American League in the World Series against the Boston Braves. Nobody in Hollywood could have written a script like that one. It was the World Series that Boston fans had dreamed about for years. All Ted Williams, Bobby Doerr, Johnny Pesky, Dom DiMaggio and company had to do was beat the Indians into submission. They didn't.

I brought my mind back to the present and looked around at the stands that were rapidly filling up for the start of the game. Looking toward the visitor's dugout along the third base line, I recognized Walt Dropo, one of my boyhood heroes from the fifties. He was wearing a black overcoat and his chiseled features were easily recognizable. I recalled our first meeting in 1950 when Mr. Dropo visited the Elks Club in St. Johnsbury and my dad took me there to meet him. I remembered how big his hands were and how powerful he looked. Forty-one years later, Walt Dropo, the "Moose" from Moosup Connecticut and the American League Rookie of the Year in 1950, still looked imposing. I told him he still looked as if he could swat the ball over the "Green Monster," as the friendly left field wall is known in baseball. Walt smiled and thanked me for the compliment. (Walt passed away in 2010 at the age of 87.) I walked toward the Red Sox dugout where John Dennis of WHDH TV was standing. I recognized him from seeing him on television a number of times. I introduced myself and asked him how many opening days he had covered.

"This will be my fifteenth, Barney, and while everything else in the world seems to change, men on the moon, space shuttles, salaries of athletes, things like that, Fenway Park doesn't seem to change. You know, that's the great thing. It's kind of like a time line that runs through the game that I don't think any other sport enjoys, pro football, hockey or even basketball. And they have mascots and halftime shooting contests and things like that. Here, there's a time line that remains constant and that kind of gives you a base on which to build. Fathers bring their sons or daughters, then they become grandfathers and great grandfathers and Fenway still looks like it did in 1912."

John's characterization of Fenway captured the history and the color of the "shrine" of baseball. There's a magical aura that surrounds Fenway Park, unlike any other sports venue, even the new Yankee Stadium with its traditions and monuments. The baseball ghosts glide through the park at their leisure, reliving their moments of glory, recreating the games they played, savoring the memories of being in the spotlight and hearing thousands of fans cheering for them. The fans are people from all walks of life who idolize many of the players because they can see themselves on the field performing heroic feats.

Fenway Park was a beautiful place to spend a warm summer afternoon, a place to get away from the stress of everyday work and raising a family. You could smell the cigar smoke drifting through the stands and you could hear the vendors: "Get your Hood's Ice Cream here." And the wonderful aroma of the peanuts....awesome. The sound of the fans singing *Take Me Out To The Ballgame*. These are some of the things I remember about being at Fenway.

My father would get very impatient with the Red Sox, at home or at the ballpark. I recall a day when dad, my brother Bob and I were at a game. The Red Sox were losing and he decided to leave in the seventh inning. Bob and I were disappointed. We made our way to the top of the Prudential Center. Sure enough, the Red Sox were staging a late inning rally and we were missing it. We looked through the 25 cent binoculars from the top of the Prudential just as Carl Yastrzemski was batting with the bases loaded. Carl popped out and dad was off the hook.

I remember going to a game in 1950 when I was on crutches because of the cast on my leg from a broken ankle suffered that summer. It was a clutch situation on the field. Vern Stephens was at bat with a chance to do some damage. When he popped one up, my dad got angry and broke one of my crutches. I limped out of the park that day using only one crutch. At home, my dad would often turn the TV set off if the Red Sox were losing. I remember watching more than a few night games after he went to bed, then telling him how the Red Sox rallied to win the game.

One of the many magical moments I enjoyed on that opening day was becoming acquainted with Scott Coen who was then the host of an evening sports talk show on WHYN in Springfield, Mass. Scott and I hit it off immediately as he picked up on the excitement I was feeling about our story and being on the field for the first time. I called Scott's show several times during that 1991 season in order to keep him updated on the progress of the book and just talk about the Red Sox. There was always something interesting to talk about. Now, in 2010, Scott is the Sports Director at Channel 40, the Fox affiliate in Springfield. He's married with a thirteen year old daughter and is enjoying his life.

After the festivities of opening day, I settled into a routine where I would phone Mary Jane Ryan in the Red Sox front office and request credentials for an upcoming game. Mary Jane and I had something in common. We were both Vermonters. She was always courteous and kind to me for the entire season.

Joanne and I were excited. There was evidence of positive thinking occurring all over the Boston area. The tulip trees were blooming along Commonwealth Avenue. Excitement and optimism abounded. It was May, the merry month of May, still very early in the season. Roger Clemens was off to a great start. The two major newspapers in Boston, the Globe and the Herald, were picking up the vision of a championship banner flying over Fenway Park for the first time in 73 years. It seemed there was a special feeling in the air and on the air. Talk show hosts and other pundits were already looking forward to the celebration that would take place in Kenmore Square where the CITGO sign flashes on and off every night. The energy level was increasing as the excitement grew and the picture of the Boston Red Sox winning the World Series became clearer. ESPN caught the vision with their baseball analysts. Peter Gammons and the Boston Globe predicted the Red Sox would win it all in 1991. Buster's All-American Bar-B-Q over on Boston's north shore exhorted the fans to come and watch the World Series at their place. Dick Powers, the editor of the Revere Journal had pinpointed the vision. He named the Red Sox opponent for the Fall Classic. Dick wrote: "Let's take care of one given for 1991. The Boston Red Sox are going to win the World Series. No more talk about it. There's nothing to talk about. Just start sucking up to your friends who have season tickets and maybe they'll invite you to a game in October when the BoSox defeat Chicago in the ALCS, and then the Dodgers for their first World championship since 1918." Nice try, Mr. Powers. You were off by thirteen years like we were.

"Make the rings and they will come." Those were the words of Gene Levanchy of WHDH as we stood on the field at Fenway on opening day. "Go down to Balfour in Attleboro," Gene said. "Get the rings printed up. Bingo! It's like Field of Dreams. Make them now. Measure the guys and get it over with. That way, they can be presented right after the game is over."

John Dennis nailed the good feelings when he and I talked about the optimism. "Well, that optimism seems to be part and parcel of what Boston fans have always been about. Even in years when they had no reason to be optimistic, they were. This year as a result of Clemens rising to the stature he has attained, I think a lot of people expect more out of this club than perhaps any in recent memory."

Dick Powers sent one of his reporters, Sandra Miller, over to our little apartment at 69 Victoria St. just to see what we were up to. The result was a very cool article about us but not a very good photo. At least, we made the front page of the Revere Journal.

Yes, The Red Sox Will Win
by Sandra Miller

 Kevin Costner in *Field of Dreams*, was told, "Build it and they will come." A pair of local authors are now urging, Think it and they will win."
 Victoria Street residents E.J. and Joanne Barney are

mixing a little New Age philosophy into the equally ancient spirit of every fan who has hoped against almost cyclical disappointment that the Red Sox win the World Series. And boy, the Sox can use all the help they can g..

"No, no, no! You mustn't think that way," he urged, the two of them jumping up in alarm. Added Joanne with a giggle. "I usually hold people down until they change their mind."

Instead of resorting to a wrestling on most of New England, however, they're collaborating on *Love Those Red Sox*, a book which could be sub-titled, *A Red Sox World Series and The Power of Positive Thinking*.

Although the Red Sox haven't won a championship since 1918, Barney has been holding out hope for another one since he was 11, sitting behind home plate with his dad during the 1948 playoff game between the Red Sox and the Cleveland Indians at Fenway Park. Shock rumbled through the ballpark when they lost 8 to 3, but the authors write in their preface, "The outcome of this game, however, did not alter my loyalty to the Red Sox. I would always remain a diehard Red Sox fan."

Barney moved from Vermont to East Boston as a boy, then back to Vermont, served twenty years in the Air Force and eventually moved to California. But every chance he had, He'd go to Fenway or keep up with the Sox and keep his Sox up.

Fans Must Think Positive To Break Bambino's Curse In 1988, Barney was a recent widower who was set up on a blind date by one of Joanne's daughters. Joanne, a retired school teacher with a doctorate in education and counseling, owned her own business, The Human Touch School of Therapeutic Massage and Healing Arts, which taught stress reduction techniques such as reflexology, acupressure and stress reduction.

"This Vermonter thought I was pretty weird," Joanne recalled. Actually, he said she challenged his whole way of looking at life.

They soon married and they both ran her business until, ironically, they found that their business was stressing them both out. So the two moved to the peaceful Mendocino community of Fort Bragg and he created a morning news and feature radio program, which trumpeted the motto, "We don't just read the news, we put people in it."

One of the guests he put into the news was his long-time baseball hero, Bobby Doerr who had recently been honored with the retirement of his number, and lived just north in Oregon.

I had wanted to call him since 1979," he says, fondly recalling the 1948-1951 killer lineup of Dom DiMaggio, Johnny Pesky, Ted Williams and Bobby Doerr.

Another turning point was the book, "Curse of The Bambino," by Globe columnist Dan Shaughnessy, which they consider a negative work that only contributes to the fan's pessimism.

Although Joanne played softball in school, she admits she's never been much of a baseball fan - heck, she admits that sometimes she gets the World Series mixed up with the Super Bowl. But she also knew that Barney should put his baseball passion to writing, and knew that she could contribute her positive thinking talents, too.

"I believe in using the sub-conscious mind and tapping into the universal," she says, trying not to sound too Shirley MacLaine-ish.

So in the middle of one particular night in March, she awoke with a revelation and woke her husband to announce, "Barney, we have to go to Winter Haven."

Barney had been noting that the Red Sox had made some particularly wise acquisitions lately with Danny Darwin and Matt Young, among others. "How could they lose?" Barney said. When I was a kid, they broke my heart. It's been what, 40 years? They are going to win this year. We have dynamite pitching, and the bats aren't coming around, but when they do, watch out."

So within a few days, he quit his job, they sold the trailer and with only a modest pension to keep a roof over their heads, they arrived in Florida with tape recorder and video camera in hands to catch the last two weeks of spring training.

The two interviewed management, athletes, the fans, the bat boys and the general "Red Sox family" that lives and breathes from April to, hopefully this year, October, all about "the attitude."

"[Manager Joe] Morgan is so laid back. He's having the time of his life. he has such talented players. They can't wait to play ball every night," Barney says. "the team thinks positive. Now, if we could get the fans to think positively....."

The couple followed the team to Boston and found a nice apartment on Victoria Street, coincidentally a ball's throw away from Macklin Field. A quick look around the apartment shows no signs of pyramids or crystals. Instead, it's sparsely decorated with a map of Revere, a Roger Clemens poster pulled from the Herald, and a paperback on "Think And Grow Rich."

Barney makes a phone call to someone in charge of allowing him access to the field, a privilege that doesn't come as easily to the Barneys as it did in Winter Haven. "They think everyone wants to publish something on the Sox," Joanne said. And they had some trouble finding a publisher before landing Desktop Publishing. At one point, they were discouraged enough to consider asking their daughter to charge their way home, but they pushed on instead. "Once you get your intent, things begin to happen," Joanne said.

On opening day, Barney made it on to the field and even inside the batter's cage. "It was spine-tingling," he recalls. "There were goosebumps on my arms. I had a vision that it was the end of the World Series and Boston had just won."

As part of his research, he goes to as many Fenway games as he can, armed with a pen, pad, tape recorder, his "bible," the 1991 Media Guide, and his lucky amethyst he wears around his neck to give the Sox an extra shot of luck, while she stays home to edit.

"This book is not just about baseball, this book is about love and faith," he explains. In one chapter of the book, they write, "The most powerful thing in the world is a THOUGHT..... How are thoughts turned into reality? By adding the emotion of desire."

In one exercise, they ask the readers to picture themselves in "the greatest ballpark in the world," pick a seat behind home plate, roam around the dugout, imagine the sights, sounds and aromas around them, give a high five to a favorite player, and generally develop a positive feeling toward the boys of summer. "From this moment on, don't let a negative thought about the Red Sox cross your mind or let a negative thought about the Red Sox from someone else go unchanged," they urge.

The book will also feature sketches by someone they ran across at Winter Haven, whom only later did they learn also has sketches hanging at the

Smithsonian - now they hope that artist George Guzzi will make a few bucks off a percentage of the proceeds.

By mid June, the book should be finished and should be on the stands next to the team yearbook by July when many fans are beginning to pay attention to the standings. The book itself will have a shelf life of only three months, they admit, but they also plan to use much of the material they couldn't fit into "Love Those Red Sox" for a biography on Doerr, for which they'll move to Oregon.

Not much can break the Barneys' optimism, not even the suggestion that by the time "Love Those Red Sox" comes out in July, the Sox will already be starting their traditional post All-Star deterioration.

"We must think positive and they will win!" Barney nearly screams. Adds Joanne: "If we believe it will happen, it will happen!" Maybe that's all the Red Sox have needed all these years - a little bit of faith.

In 1991, we had a much smaller vision of this story. We had no way of knowing that many medical problems would arise and get in the way of being a would-be-author. Of course, we didn't know that positive thinking would take hold in New England and some new owners would instill a winning attitude in the Red Sox players. Oh yes, they hired a manager named Terry Francona and a GM named Theo Epstein. Enough said.

FIVE

The biggest event of the 1991 season was scheduled for the weekend of May 11th and 12th, coinciding with Mother's Day. On Saturday, there would be an Old-Timers' game and on Sunday, Ted Williams would be honored for hitting .406 in 1941, the golden anniversary of the record that still stands.

Most big league ballplayers will tell you that baseball is essentially a game of constant failure. If a player is consistently able to succeed three times out of every ten chances at bat, he is doing very good. His batting average would be .300. To get four hits every ten at bats over the course of an entire season is a phenomenal achievement. In 1941, Ted came to bat 456 times. He got 185 hits and walked 145 times, the same as the year before. In that amazing 1941 season, Ted struck out only 27 times. He really had his eye on the ball.

Will the record ever be broken? In 1941, most of the games were played during the day and teams only had to travel as far west as St. Louis. Pitchers generally stayed in games for seven, eight or even nine innings. Today, hitters may see three or four pitchers per game. A complete game is a rarity. There is a middle inning reliever, a set-up man and a closer in every team's bullpen. In other words, the chances of anyone hitting over .400 for 162 games is remote. The same thing could be said for Joe DiMaggio's 56 game hitting streak also accomplished in 1941. I do not believe that streak will ever be equaled.

Ted Williams finished his illustrious career with 521 home runs. Consider this. He missed three years during World War II and another two seasons during the Korean War. Imagine how many home runs he would have hit if he had played five more full seasons. I believe the number would have been 200 or more. In 1957 at the age of 39, Ted hit .388 and won another batting title. He won one more batting title in 1958, giving him a total of six for his career.

I started following Ted's career when I was ten years old. My dad used to bring home the old Boston Post and I would clip articles and cartoons about the Red Sox and Braves players. I remember writing to Ted one year about his baseball camp. I never attended but I did get a black and white autographed photo of him swinging a bat. I saw Ted play in a lot of games at Fenway from 1946 to 1960. It seemed that we were always late getting to the park and we would miss the Red Sox taking batting or fielding practice. I loved watching Ted, even if he was practicing. He was always grinning and looking very relaxed during warm up drills. He was my idol and now in 1991, I was on the field at the same time he was. Ted was obviously enjoying himself. He was dressed casually in a khaki outfit, had a big smile on his tanned facial features and was taking great delight in the camaraderie with friends and former team-mates. His lovely daughter, Claudia, was also on the field. I learned that she was going to school in Vermont. Claudia told me she sometimes wished she had been a boy so she could have played catch with her father. I told Claudia about our project and how I would be thrilled to talk to him. She said she would mention me to him.

The big guy was asking a television producer what he was supposed to do as people filling the stands cried out, "Ted, Ted." He was approached by Lynne nelson, a freelance writer like me. She asked Ted how he felt about being there. Since I was standing beside her, I switched on my Sony recorder.

His voice was strong and resonant. "Well, it's certainly a big thrill for me to be back at Fenway. I sort of hope this will be the last time because there's always something I have to do to come here eventually though I enjoy it. You know, I don't want to wear myself out, from the fans thinking about me. I'm going to have a good time here today because I'm going to see a lot of my teammates. Joe DiMaggio's here. I have great respect and admiration for him. His brother Dom is here. Johnny and Bobby are here and little Billy Klaus is here, so it will be a great day."

"As John Henry gets older, this will be a special moment for both of you to share," said Lynne.

"Yeah, we'll have it on film," Ted answered. Lynne Nelson thanked Ted and suddenly it was my turn to talk to my hero, who, in my eyes, was the greatest baseball player ever to play the game. I had idolized Ted since I was eight years old and now, forty-six years later, I was standing in front of him, wearing my Red Sox baseball cap and feeling a little nervous.

"Ted, would you please say a word about Bobby Doerr. My wife and are writing a book and part of it is a tribute to Bobby."

Ted smiled that big famous Ted Williams smile. "Oh, Bobby Doerr. I can't say enough about him. He is my closest personal friend that I've known longer than anyone else in professional baseball. I have so much respect for him. I don't know how I could feel any more deeply than I do for Bobby Doerr."

"You often called him the Captain," I said to Ted. Ted laughed. 'Yeah, I gave him that captain stuff."

Another gentleman was standing beside me, anxious to get a sound bite from Ted. I let my tape keep rolling.

"Mickey Owen was telling me a great story around the batting cage," the man said to Ted. "He ended his career with the Red Sox in 1954. He said he hit the ultimate home run, two outs, bottom of the ninth, three runs down. They walked you to load the bases, then he hits it out."

Ted flashed a big grin. "Oh baby. Yeah, I remember that one. Great guy. Listen, I got to go."

"Are you going to get some fishing in," I called out to my hero. "I'm going to, I hope, in a couple of months."

Ted Williams loved fishing, from the lakes and streams of Maine, down to the blue waters of the Florida Keys. He absolutely loved visiting Bobby Doerr so the two best friends could spend leisurely time up on the spectacular Rogue River where Bobby had a cabin. Williams was a perfectionist. He had to be the best at everything he did, hitting a baseball, flying jets or tying flies. Being the best included fly-casting or fishing for Florida Marlin. Ted and his close personal friend, the late Curt Gowdy, one of Wyoming's favorite sons and the former voice of the Red Sox, teamed up to make dozens of fishing shows for "Wide World of Sports" on ABC. Some people said Ted Williams would rather be fishing than playing baseball.

In the November 25th, 1996 issue of Sports Illustrated with Ted on the cover, there is a marvelous article on his life and the hell of growing old. He was 78 when S.L. Price wrote the story. Near the end of the article, Ted told a fishing story.

"He speaks about his refuge on the Kiamichi River in New Brunswick, Canada, and about spending hours tying thousands of flies and about the throat-catching moment after you've cast the fly and played the fish and you feel the hook dig in. Talking about fishing is not like talking about baseball or politics or history. No, Williams calls what he did in the water "a privilege" and lowers his voice as if describing something holy. And he keeps coming back to the same fish, that 35-pound salmon he hooked 3 1/2 years ago on Quebec's Cascapedia River. It was the middle of the day. "Jeez, what a place!" he says. "Only kings and presidents and big shots and billionaires get to fish there."

It was as big a salmon as he ever fought. "I made a helluva good cast because I was in kind of a narrow spot, and I was picking at it," he says. His hand slices back and forth across the kitchen table as if it were the surface of the river. His face is alight. "Picking at it this way, and I'm shooting it that way! I was casting 60, 70 feet - a dry fly – and he took it."

Williams leans forward, sets his feet and bears down. His face reddens. "And I fought him," he growls. His voice drops, goes soft as goose down. "And I fought him a little harder. And I fought him really hard. I'm thinking. Jeez, I can't bring this fish home, and I'm really flossing it to him, see! And it's a deep little run there. He was down maybe 10 feet, and I couldn't see him.....and I'm really lifting him up! Ummmmmph!" He has an invisible fly rod in his hands, and he's trying like hell to pull the fish up through the kitchen floor, his face screwed up from the strain.

"And then I let go," he says. The invisible rod drops. He crooks a finger in his mouth and tugs. "I had hooked him on this big, dry single hook and I was just pulling him too hard! I tried the hard pull and he didn't break, so with a good bend I dragged him right up, and the hook pulled out just as he came out of the water." The salmon dropped with a splash. Gone.

It's over. Ted Williams comes back to himself, to a chair in the kitchen, with a fish show on TV. "I didn't get him," he says, "I'll always remember that moment when I close my eyes." He is asked to name the river again, and he repeats it: Cascapedia.

"The closest place to heaven I'll ever be," he says. "I know that."

At the end of his baseball career, Ted tried his hand at managing, at the impassioned plea of his close friend, Robert Short, the owner of the Washington Senators which later became the Texas Rangers. Additionally, he signed on as a consultant for Sears & Roebuck, affixing his signature to a long line of fishing equipment and other sporting goods. Ted's foray into managing a major league team lasted for two years. He managed the Senators, then the Rangers for one year before resigning, much to the chagrin of his friend Short. I do not have knowledge of Ted's managing experiences but I feel certain he didn't have the patience to teach fundamental baseball to young prospects and he couldn't tolerate losing. He was such a perfectionist and when he saw flaws in his managing techniques, he just threw in the towel and went back to fishing where he could be one with nature and just decide where to cast the next lure.

The fans that came to Fenway Park on Sunday, May 12th, 1991, were given a large, commemorative folder, a beautiful color depiction of Ted's career highlights. On the field, the original assemblage was on an easel, under glass. There were folding chairs facing home plate for assembled guests. Mrs. Jean Yawkey was seated to the right of Ted. It would be her final public appearance. The emcee for the event was Curt Gowdy and when he introduced Ted, the appreciative roar from the crowd nearly drowned out his words. I was kneeling in front of Ted along with several other photographers. I had a 35 millimeter Minolta single lens reflex camera ready to take a great picture.

Ted, dressed in a gray sport jacket, a light blue shirt and dark blue trousers, stepped up to the microphone. His words echoed through the caverns and canyons of the old ball yard.

"When they first told me they were going to do this, I tried to think of what I should do and I finally realized that after all these years, I should tip my hat to the greatest fans on earth." I took the photo just as he raised his cap. The 30,000 or so fans in attendance gave Ted a long standing ovation. It was a "goose bump" moment at Fenway.

Later, we learned he had borrowed the cap from Jeff Reardon, a Red Sox relief pitcher. As the crowd quieted, Ted continued speaking.

"I realized I was playing for super great fans. I had a love affair with them but I never showed it. When I finally consented to do this day in my honor, I started to think: What am I going to say? Then I thought it would be nice to tip my cap."

Ted got another standing ovation from the fans, many of whom remembered how the Boston sportswriters would get on his case for never tipping his cap when he rounded the bases after hitting a home run. They got on him for refusing to wear a necktie to social functions. What was not publicized were Ted's charitable donations, the time he spent with kids in hospitals and his many friendships with waitresses, bellhops and even peanut vendors. He loved the people from all walks of life, even the guy inside the wall at Fenway who would put the numbers on the scoreboard. Ted loved talking to him.

He was sometimes temperamental, once flinging his bat up on to the protective screen behind home plate, then climbing the screen to get it back. Another time, he gave booing fans a "french salute," as a photographer from the Boston Post snapped a picture.

In my mind and thousands of adoring fans, Ted Williams could do no wrong. He was an American hero on the baseball field and in the cockpits of fighter planes in two wars where he served with distinction. When the U.S. Marines needed a damned good fighter pilot to help out in Korea, they knew exactly who to call and they knew that Ted would not complain. Mr. Bob Hanna of a newspaper called the Standard Times wrote a wonderful article about an incident in Korea that nearly took Ted's life. The article follows:

Dateline - 1995

Last Thursday, America paid tribute to the Korean War veterans. Finally.

That must have pleased one Theodore Samuel Williams, one of the 1.5 million Americans who served in Korea, who also earned a fair amount of distinction in a baseball uniform. A captain in the reserves, Williams had been called back to active duty because the Marines were short on pilots and shorter on time to train new ones.

Most of us know about the game winning home run he hit in his last at bat before reporting for duty, and the home run he hit on his second at bat when he returned, but few of us knew what went on in those intervening years. I knew he landed a burning plane once, (My note: it happened on February 17th, 1953, my 16th birthday) but was unfamiliar with the details until reading Ed Linn's book: "Hitter, The Life and Turmoils of Ted Williams." For those of you who have not read the book, his exploits in Korea are worth a mention.

For instance, did you know that his squadron leader in Korea was John Glenn? Yes, the former astronaut and now U.S. Senator from Ohio. Williams flew 39 combat missions in Korea, the last half of them as Glenn's wingman, meaning he was the best and most trusted pilot in the squadron. As good as Williams was with the bat, he was equally as good with a stick in a cockpit.

Red Sox teammate Johnny Pesky, who went to preflight training school with Williams in chapel Hill, N. Carolina, had this to say in the book about Williams' flying and target shooting at the Pensacola training base in Florida.

"I heard he literally tore the sleeve target to shreds with his angle dives. He'd shoot from wingovers, zooms and barrel rolls, and after a few passes, the sleeve was in ribbons. At any rate, I know he broke the all-time record for hits."

From Pensacola, Williams was sent to Jacksonville for an advanced course in air gunnery where he broke all existing records for reflexes, coordination and visual reaction time.

"From what I heard," Pesky said, "Ted could make a plane and its six pianos (machine guns) play like a symphony orchestra.

But all that experience and skill nearly went down in flames in Korea.

"I was on a strike at a troop encampment near Kyomipo," said Williams. "The funny thing was I didn't feel anything. I knew I was hit when the stick started shaking like mad in my hands. Then everything went out, my radio, my landing gear, everything. The red warning lights were on all over the plane."

The F9 Panther jet was now trailing smoke and fire. Other pilots in Williams' squadron were yelling for him to eject, but his radio was dead and he couldn't see the flames in back of his plane.

Before losing his radio entirely, he was able to send out a mayday and receive some instructions from another pilot who came alongside his jet and guided him to the nearest airport.

"Larry Hawkins," Williams said. "A young Lieutenant from

Pennsylvania. He saved my life."

But it wasn't that simple. Williams' landing gear, remember, was jammed and Hawkins was frantically trying to signal Williams to eject as they approached the landing strip.

"But I decided to ride my plane in," said Williams. "If I knew then my plane was on fire, I damn well would have shot the canopy and jumped. I came barreling in at more than 200 miles an hour, fighting the stick all the way. Nothing worked, no dive brakes, no flaps, nothing to slow up the plane."

"Then I heard a hollow "whoomph" behind me."

That was the flames, spreading to engulf the entire aircraft as Williams came in for a belly landing, skidding some two or three thousand feet.

"I thought I'd never stop," said Williams. "When I did, I released the canopy and almost fell out."

And then he ran as fast as his long legs would carry him, just moments before the plane exploded. Williams estimated that he had only about 20 or 30 seconds worth of fuel left. A minute tops, but it was only because the plane was out of fuel that it didn't blow up when it hit the runway. How's that for passing through a narrow window?

But Williams didn't have time to dwell on that. The next day, he was up in the air again, on another mission.

Ted returned from the war years in 1946 and helped lead the Red Sox to the American League championship, after which he played in his only World Series and was a non-factor as the team lost to the Cardinals in seven games. The closest he came to being in another World Series was in 1948 when Gene Bearden's knuckleball baffled Red Sox hitters. In 1949, they were beaten out by the hated Yankees on the final weekend of the season. That was the year that Ted made headlines by signing a contract worth $100,000 per season that made him the highest paid player in baseball.

A photo of me interviewing Ted appeared on the front page of the Boston Globe Northeastern edition on Sunday, May 12th, 1991. My brother called me from his home in Andover, Mass. to tell me about the picture. I never saw it. Now, in 2010, I intend to track it down.

Ted Williams passed away on July 5th, 2002 at the age of 83. He is gone but will never be forgotten. The Ted Williams tunnel in Boston stands out as a lasting memorial and there's a statue outside of Fenway Park. His record feat of hitting .406 will stand out for the ages and the hundreds of photographs will keep Ted in the hearts of his adoring fans forever.

Six

Hall of Famer Bobby Doerr lives in Junction City, Oregon and his telephone number is listed in local phone books. I always wanted to call him and talk about his playing days so when I went to work for KSAY, I had the opportunity to do that. What follows is the chat we had on the air and the story of Joanne and I meeting Bobby and his wife in person.

He wore the uniform with the number "1" and he was the regular second baseman for the Red Sox from 1937 until 1952 when back problems forced him into early retirement from the game he loved so much. Bobby was my dad's favorite player and everybody's favorite player. He was a ballplayer with a wonderful reputation for being a kind and gentle man who knew how to play the game of baseball.

Bobby was elected to the Hall of Fame in 1987. I was curious to know why it took so long for his talents to be recognized by the writers who do the voting every year.

"My feeling was that for a number of years, it was outfielders and first basemen going in with the exception of Rogers Hornsby," Bobby said. "There were very few middle infielders. The guys with the offensive stats were getting in, then they started putting some infielders in like Lou Boudreau and Luis Aparicio. It's nice nowadays to see guys like Ryne Sandberg coming along. He's a good looking young infielder."

I explained to Bobby that I was excited about putting a story together about the Red Sox, one that would not focus on the negative history and the disappointments but rather on the great legacy left by players like himself, Johnny Pesky, Dom DiMaggio and Ted Williams, the heroes that live forever in the hearts of their fans.

"Well that would be alright," Bobby said. "It seems when I look back on all the things that happened in my baseball career, I was lucky to be in a World Series and All Star games and get voted into the Hall of Fame and to have my number retired and so on but the biggest regret was that they didn't get to play on a winning World Series team. You look back and in '46, we had Ferriss win 25, Hughson with 20, Mickey Harris wins 17 and all three of them come down with sore arms in '47.

"If just one of them hadn't got a sore arm, we should have won in '49 and '50. What we needed was a specialized relief pitcher, but that took a starting pitcher away, so we were always just one pitcher short. Of course, the Yankees had Joe Page. Imagine all the games he came in and saved."

I shared my own memories of how I felt about the great Yankee relief pitcher, how I would feel physically sick when Page came out of the bullpen and shut down the Red Sox hitters.

"Was it psychological, Bobby?" "When you went into Yankee Stadium, did you feel any change? Did you tighten up?"

"Well, no we didn't," Bobby answered, "but god, that's the worst place in the world for a right hander to hit in. You had a long left field fence. If you hit a ball, you knew it was just a big out. They always had the white shirts down in center field and you had to look at them, then there were the late afternoon shadows across the field to deal with." Bobby laughed. "Yankee Stadium was never a fun place for me."

Bobby and I talked about the Yankees pitching staff.

"They had some good pitchers," Bobby said. "But they weren't like a Cleveland or Detroit pitching staff. They were good but they weren't that good if you know what I mean. The big thing was, we had so much right handed hitting and they just pitched around Ted quite a bit. It was just one of those things. When we finished tied in '48 then one game out in '49, we weren't that bad. You can look back earlier. If we had that one specialized relief pitcher like the Yankees had, we probably would have won eight to ten more games per year."

Bobby Doerr played in nine All-Star games. I asked him which one stood out.

"It was 1943. I hit a home run with two men on. We won the game. It was five to three or something like that. I hit it off Mort Cooper. It was a high hanging curve ball. First time up! I'll remember it as long as I live. It was something a pitcher would like to run up and grab and take back if they could. I was lucky."

I was having such a good time talking to this great player. In my mind, I could see him playing second base at Fenway Park and standing in the batters' box. Bobby had a swing that was tailor-made for the inviting left field fence. I asked Bobby what position he liked hitting in the most.

"Well, I hit fourth sometimes. See, Ted would hit third and when I was going good, sometimes I would hit cleanup and when Vern Stephens came over, I moved to fifth. (Vern came to the Red Sox in a trade that sent Jack Cramer to St. Louis.) Vern was a good ballplayer, I'll tell you. he was a good shortstop and he'd drive in a hundred and forty or fifty runs a season for us."

Time was running short and I wanted to ask Bobby about fishing.

Bobby Doerr and Ted Williams shared a common interest away from the baseball fields and that was fishing. Whenever possible, Ted would come to Oregon and the two men would travel up to the wild and beautiful Rogue River. I wanted to know if Bobby tied his own flies.

"I don't make my own flies," Bobby said. "I'm just not patient enough to tie them. I fly fish a lot but I just never have really got into tying flies. Ted just loves it. He's real good. He's one of the world's great fishermen just as he was the world's greatest hitter. He is the best, really. Anything he does, he's going to do well."

Ted Williams was not shy in expressing his love and respect for Bob Doerr like so many other people in baseball. Jerry Remy, a former Red Sox second baseman, is a color commentator for NESN, the New

England Sports Network. Today, Jerry is proud to work with Don Orsillo on every Red Sox telecast and he is the very popular presidents of Red Sox Nation. I met Jerry in Winter Haven and we had lunch together. I asked him to share his thoughts on Bobby.

"Bobby Doerr is a class guy," Jerry said. "You meet him once and you feel as if you've known him your whole life. I've got a picture at home I had taken with he and Johnny Pesky. It's a picture I keep on my wall with Doerr being a Hall of Famer and Pesky a long time Red Sox great. It was an honor for me to be in that picture. The thing that sticks with me is what kind of guy Doerr is. I don't know much about his playing time. That was before my time, although my father tells me he was quite a player. It may have taken him a long time to get to the Hall of fame but he got there. That's the most important thing. A lot of guys don't even get a sniff, but he got in and it couldn't have happened to a nicer guy."

John McLaren was serving as the bullpen coach for the Red Sox in 1991 after being with the Toronto organization for five years. John gave me his thoughts on Bobby.

"Oh god, he's one of my all time favorites. When I first started with Toronto, he was a major league hitting coach and then he came down to the minors as a hitting instructor. He kind of took me under his wing a little bit. He taught me about patience. Bobby Doerr always found something good to say about everybody. All the minor league kids loved him. He's a great guy. He and Monica (Mrs. Doerr) are really good people. I can remember him telling me stories about Fenway Park, about Ted and Johnny Pesky. Bobby is such a good person to have around. He always seemed to have a gleam in his eye and have something positive to say, never moody or complaining about anything. I can remember when Bobby would come around to the minor league teams and we would go out to lunch or go out after a game and he would talk about Williams telling him, 'Bobby, you can't hit like that. You can't do that,' and Bobby would say, 'But, Ted, I'm not like you. I don't have the eyes you have or the magic in my bat like you have.'"

John and I laughed. We could both see Bobby almost pleading with

Ted in his good-natured manner. John continued talking about Bobby. "Lloyd Moseby of the Blue Jays just loves him as so many people do. He's one in a million, Barney." I thanked John for sharing his thoughts of Bobby.

When Joanne and I got to meet the Doerrs in person, we discovered they were an extraordinarily devoted couple. Bobby and I had made previous arrangements to meet in the lobby of the Sheraton Hotel in Boston. Would he find us? I had called his room and left a message that we were in the lobby. Then, moments later, I saw him walking toward us from the elevator. I recognized him immediately. I was so excited that I shook hands with Bobby twice.

He was wearing a powder blue sport coat with a dark blue turtleneck sweater and his bright blue eyes sparkled as I introduced him to Joanne. I felt so proud to have her standing beside me, supporting me as I realized a cherished boyhood dream of meeting one of my heroes in person. As the three of us chatted, a man brought his young son over to where we were standing.

"Mr. Doerr, may I have your autograph?" the boy said to Bobby.

Bobby asked the boy for his name, then signed a color photo of himself that the boy handed to him. It was obvious that the youngster was thrilled.

"Let's go up to the room where we can talk some more," Bobby said to us. The three of us took the elevator to the fifteenth floor, then walked down the hallway to the room where Mrs. Doerr was waiting.

Monica Doerr was a beautiful lady. Her hair was silver white and her face glowed with admiration for her husband. I recalled her response when I first called Bobby earlier in 1991. When I told her Bobby was my favorite player and asked to speak to him, she said: "How nice of you to remember."

The two of them met in Oregon in 1937, the year I was born. They were married in 1938. Mrs. Doerr was now suffering from Multiple Sclerosis and had to use a wheel chair. Traveling with her husband involved a lot of special preparations and accommodations but the two of them were inseparable.

I had to stay focused as Bobby and I talked baseball. Even though I was seated, I felt I was a few feet off the ground, having a face to face conversation with a Boston Red Sox Hall of Fame player! As Bobby and I conversed, it was as if I had known him for many years and in a way, I had, through the magic of baseball and boyhood idols. I thought about my father and how much he loved the Red Sox and how he would have enjoyed being there with his favorite player.

Joanne sat on the side of the bed visiting with Mrs. Doerr about families. Bobby and I were watching the telecast of the game with the Texas rangers that was going on at Fenway Park, just a short distance from the Sheraton. We were analyzing each player's strengths and weaknesses as they came to the plate or made a play in the field. Again, I had to stay focused. Here I was in a hotel room with a Hall of Fame player. Me, an ordinary Red Sox fan from Vermont. It was a spine-tingling experience that's etched in my memory.

Too soon, it seemed, the evening was over. We exchanged hugs with the Doerrs, explaining that we preferred hugs to handshakes. Bobby set us at ease immediately by sharing personal memories of growing up in a family that shared lots of hugs. We thanked Bobby and Monica and said we would look forward to seeing them at Fenway Park the next day for the old-timer's day celebration.

At Fenway the next day, I asked Johnny Pesky to share a favorite story about Bobby. He smiled as he answered.

"Barney, I was put with Bobby by Joe Cronin during my rookie year. We roomed together, often ate together and we would always talk baseball. When we went on the road, we would talk about things that could happen. If we were going to play the White Sox, we'd analyze the players to see who hits and runs, who steals, what pitchers had the best moves and so on. After my rookie year, we all went into the service. That's when I took up smoking cigars. I'll never forget Bobby telling me the story of how much Mrs. Doerr disliked the smell. On the road, we would have the windows closed and the cigars going."

"When we returned home, Mrs. Doerr asked Bobby who he was rooming with and she wanted to know if he smoked. 'Yeah, those cigars,' Bobby tells her."

"So finally, when we were on the road, I'd have to smoke outside the room. You know, Barney, Bobby is one of those guys who never did anything malicious in his whole life, having a drink, cussing or whatever. In those years, he was just one of the greatest players of our time. Of course, Williams got all the accolades, DiMaggio with the Yankees and Musial with the Cardinals. Bobby Doerr was as good a player that ever played the game."

Johnny smiled. "When you talk about Bobby Doerr, you're talking about a high class guy who was not only a good player but a great player. If you ever spend any time around him, you can't help but see what a good person he is. You often wonder how your kids are going to turn out. You hope your children grow up to be half the person he is."

I would have the extraordinarily great pleasure of being with Bobby Doerr and Johnny Pesky on a baseball field when I attended Red Sox Fantasy Camp in 1994. Then as in that dream come true season of 1991, Bobby Doerr simply reinforced what I already knew. In the hearts and minds of Red Sox fans everywhere in the nation, Bobby Doerr is truly "Number One."

Seven

In my personal collection of baseball memorabilia is a ball signed by Johnny Pesky, congratulating me for getting my first hit at Fantasy Camp. I treasure that baseball as I treasure the friendship of this great gentleman.

I call Johnny "A man for all seasons" because he exemplifies the extraordinary qualities of a famous major league baseball player who is one of the most affable and amiable persons in the world. I am so honored to be his friend. When the Boston Red Sox clinched the World Series victory in St. Louis in 2004, they rushed down to the clubhouse and handed the trophy to Johnny who was already drenched in champagne and tears. He held the splendid trophy above his head and said; "This one's for you, Ted." Johnny Pesky had waited patiently for 58 years for redemption and it could not have been sweeter for him. He was grateful.

Incredibly, Johnny has served the Red Sox for more than seventy years as a player, a coach, a manager, a broadcaster, a scout, an advisor and an ambassador. He's the go-to guy when the ball club needs something. The ball club had already given the right field foul pole to Johnny and then in 2008, they decided to add his uniform number 6 to the right field facade. Number 1 belongs to Bobby Doerr. Number 4 was worn by Joe Cronin. Number 8 was Hall of Famer Carl "Yaz" Yastrzemski. Number 9 represents Ted Williams. Carlton Fisk wore number 27 and finally, Jackie Robinson's number, honored in every major league ballpark, was 42. The most recent number to be retired at Fenway Park is 14, belonging to new Hall of Famer, Jim Rice.

Johnny would be the first to tell you he doesn't deserve all that. After all, he's just doing his job for Messrs. John Henry, Tom Werner, Larry Lucchino and Theo Epstein.

Johnny was waiting for me in sunny Fenway Park on a June afternoon in 1991. He had graciously consented to a one-on-one interview and I was fifteen minutes tardy for the appointment. "You're late, Barn," he said to me. I mumbled an apology, blaming the "T", then sat down beside him and turned on the tape recorder.

Johnny has breakfast with his pals every morning. They don't solve all the world's problems, he told me with a laugh. I wanted to know about his relationship with Tom Yawkey, the former owner of the Red Sox.

"We were all family to him, Barney. One time just before I left for the Navy, I came into the clubhouse and there was a note on my chair asking me to go upstairs and see Mr. Collins, the general manager. My batting average was right up there and I was playing well. I had no idea what he wanted. Williams is sitting in his cubicle and says, 'Go on up there and see what he wants.' So I go upstairs and Mr. Collins hands me an envelope, saying, 'You're a good kid, John. We like you. We thought you could use this.' I get back downstairs and Williams is excited. 'Open it up, for crissake,' Ted says to me. Well I open it and there's a check for $5,000 inside. That was their way of showing their appreciation. Hell, I was only making four grand a year. 'Dammit, Johnny, you're worth it,' Ted says to me with a big grin. I'll tell you. It was a hell of a nice surprise."

"How long are you going to be around?" Johnny asked me.

I told him I planned to stay for the entire season. He grinned and looked at me with a twinkle in his eyes. "We brought Mo Vaughn up from Pawtucket today."

I got excited. I let out a whoop of joy, pumping my fist in the air, much to Johnny's amusement. Mo was displaying awesome power at the AAA level, just as he had done in spring training. I knew he must have been eager to get to Fenway.

"Well, anyway, we'll see how he handles it," Johnny said. "I'm sure he'll handle it well. We need that bat in the lineup. Maybe he will. Maybe he won't. We're going to find out. I have a good feeling about that kid."

"Oh, he'll be pumped up," I said to Johnny.

"Yeah, Barn. He's in the clubhouse. He's playing tonight."

The Red Sox were facing the Yankees in the opener of a three-game series. I had already made arrangements to get credentials for the game and I had John Lesniewski, my niece's husband, signed on as my photographer. John and I were in the Red Sox dugout before the game that night. I was able to get a comment from a very excited Mo Vaughn. I asked him how he felt inside.

"I don't get too high and I don't get too low. I'm somewhere in the middle and I just want to help the team."

Despite all the hoopla and the optimism, the game turned into a Titanic-like disaster. The Yankees had an 8 to 0 lead by the fourth inning and John left early because he had to travel back to Providence. Big Mo collected his first hit, a single, and the Fenway faithful gave him a rousing reception.

Back to Fenway with Johnny. "I love it," I said.

"Yeah, you get all excited but the other guy has done a decent job."

The other guy was Carlos Quintana of Venezuela who was enjoying a good season and delivering some clutch base hits. His very promising career was later cut short by an automobile accident and Carlos was released in 1994.

"We'll see what happens," Pesky continued. "This is too good a team. We're only three games over .500. We should be ten or twelve over by this time. Toronto made a big trade, you know. They gave up two pretty good players, Glenallen Hill and Mark Whitten for Tom Candiotti. Everybody wants to win but you have to pay the price."

I gave Johnny an update on the progress of our story. "We're doing a chapter on Bobby Doerr and I know you must have a story about your playing days together that stands out above all the others." I told

Johnny I would like to hear that story, then focus on his career with the Red Sox.

"We had the old clubhouse, Barney. I was next to Williams and he always dressed next to Dominic. There was Ted, Paul Schrieber, who was our pitching coach and then me. The when Vern Stephens came over from the Browns, he was next to me. You reach three feet and you could touch one another. Our clubhouses weren't as big as they are today. Bobby was very quiet, both he and Dominic. We'd come out and do our work. I always warmed up with Bobby before he took infield practice. He was a good hitter, a great hitter. I remember how he was struggling right after the war. Course, Ted's hitting about .600 and Dominic's hitting .400 and I'm in the same area. We're all sitting in the dugout. Ted was over by the tarpaulin having some pictures taken for a magazine or something.

"Here comes Ted, all of a sudden.

"'Hey, Bobby,' he says. 'Get your bat. Come on up here.'

"'One day, you're open,' Ted says to Bobby. 'One day you're closed. Your feet are together or wide apart. You're holding your bat up high or low. My god, get a stance, then go from there.'

"Bobby, good as gold, says, 'Well, Ted, I'm not you. I can't do the things you do.'

"Williams throws his arms up in the air and says loudly, 'You want to be a .280 hitter. Be a lousy .280 hitter.'"

I laughed at the story. It sounded like a typical Ted Williams good-natured chiding of his good friend.

"But Barney," Johnny continued. "Bobby hit thirty home runs that year. They had such talent: Doerr, Williams, DiMaggio, people like that. You know, it's a simple game, but sometimes very difficult to play. God gives those kind of guys exceptional talents and you have to include Bobby in that. he was always a great talent but a great human being first. In the years that we played, there was a closeness between Ted, Dominic, Bobby and myself and maybe our pitching coach, Paul Schrieber. These were great people. Attitude and respect were always there."

I asked Johnny to compare the attitudes in the forties with attitudes in the nineties. He had an interesting answer.

"I think there are a few players today that love the game as much as we did but it's much more difficult to play today because of the expansion. The years that we played, we only went as far as St. Louis and Chicago. A lot of people don't understand that. We used to go by train, then we started flying which was great. The trains gave us a little more time with one another. From Boston to New York, for example, we'd say, 'Who's pitching tomorrow?' We'd go over what he does, how he threw the ball and things of that sort. You can learn something in fifteen or twenty minutes but when you continually say something about a person, you get an idea what he's like, especially on the field. There were guys we had an utter dislike for until we were on the same club with them and got to know them."

I immediately thought of the Yankees and my own boyhood attitudes. The Yankees always seemed to find a way to beat the Red Sox. I dislike them intensely even though I didn't know them personally. I asked Johnny how he felt about the Yankees players.

"You know, Barney, they said we hated the Yankees. I think that's kind of a cliché. I hated the Yankees and maybe outwardly I would hate them. Inwardly, I had great respect and admiration for them."

"They always brought out the best in you didn't they, Johnny?"

"Oh sure and you busted your hump a little bit more than you normally would. You played hard against everybody but the Yankees in those years were the top dog. They were winning pennant after pennant. They had great people. It was respect we felt but we earned the same respect from them too."

David Halberstam wrote in *Summer of '49,* the marvelous story about the Yankees - Red Sox exciting season, that Tommy Henrich told him "the Yankees had to win a lot of pennants so they could earn as much money as Mr. Yawkey was paying his Red Sox players." I asked Johnny to comment on that statement.

"I don't believe that, Barney. It's a different ball of wax nowadays. Ownership comes into the picture. In those days, we played for a single owner, Mr. Yawkey here, Mr. Barrow in New York, Mr. Mack in Philadelphia, Mr. Griffith in Washington, Mr. Briggs in Detroit, Chomsky in Chicago, Veeck in Cleveland and the DeWitts in St. Louis. You only had eight teams. We played each team twenty-two times a year, eleven there and eleven at home."

Johnny continued. "The thing about those years was that we played Tuesday through Saturday, then a doubleheader on Sunday, then Monday off. The first year and a half here, we never had lights. New York had lights. We were one of the last ones in the majors to get lights. That's the way it was. Now, fifty years have flown by and everything is so different. Everything happens so fast today. Life moves at a faster pace. Every day you pick up a paper, somebody is being pulled over for going over the speed limit and you just hope that no one gets killed at those great rates of speed. It's a whole different thing. I think everything is better these days. Somebody said to me just the other day, 'Don't you wish you were playing today?'

"Well, sure, but I wish I was 26 or 27 years old and had a little baseball experience. Knowing what I know from being a youngster, I'm for the player, really and the owners are for the player because television's come in and radio and we have a big marketing department now and I think everything's better. I ask them; Would you like to live the way you did twenty or thirty years ago? Of course not. You've got a better house. You have better facilities and air conditioning now, if you have the funds for it. In those days, we did everything a little at a time. If you needed a new roof or some windows or a door, you couldn't just go out and do it all in one whack because you had to rob Peter to pay Paul and the most important thing was to feed your family. That's how we were taught. We had some value for a dollar. We probably spend as much money now because everything is so expensive. Years ago, you could get a great steak for five bucks or so. Now, it's what, twenty or thirty dollars? If you have a Chateaubriand, that's forty bucks or if you have lobster. Course, everyone wants to live well and you can understand that."

Johnny was alluding to inflation and the erosion of the dollar over the years. The benchmark for comparing prices is generally 1967. Twenty dollars bought a lot more in 1967 than it does now. The cost of a basket of groceries has probably tripled or quadrupled from then until now. The salaries of athletes are outlandish. A .250 hitter can become a multi-millionaire after one season, depending what market he's playing in. New York, Chicago and the San Francisco Bay Area are the only markets supporting two teams, though Oakland has struggled for years. Kansas City, Seattle, Pittsburgh, Baltimore, and Washington continue to try and keep their heads above water while L.A., Boston and the Yankees rein in the best players. The Tampa Bay Rays have a good foundation but their fan support is shaky because there are so many other things to do in that area of Florida. Will the salaries ever be based on performance? Will there be a cap on what a player can earn? Doubtful.

Sitting there in sunny Fenway Park was exhilarating. We were both relaxed and enjoying talking to each other. I asked Johnny to share recollections about going to the movies when the team was on the road.

"Were John Wayne and Jimmy Stewart your favorites, Johnny?"

"Oh yes, Wayne and of course, we liked Stewart. William Holden, Cary Grant, Clark Gable and Tyrone Power were other favorites. I was on a base with Tyrone Power when I was in the Navy. He was a Marine flier. I never got to meet him but the girls would chase him up and down the streets on base. He seemed like a pleasant guy. Taylor (Robert Taylor) was another one. See, Barney, the war changed a lot of things around for a lot of people. It made them aware that life is very, very important. We have good doctors now. They've cured a lot of people."

I asked Johnny about his own health problems.

"Yeah, I became allergic to, of all things, flour and wheat. I thought I had cancer but the doctor assured me I didn't. I get two physicals a year, one in February, one in June. I just got my second one the other day and the doctor said everything is fine. He told me to just keep doing what I'm doing. I can't have anything like a beer or whiskey. Brandy has a nice taste. My system can tolerate that."

I told Johnny he looked good. He had good color and lots of energy. As I write about my dear friend, I think about him and just today, the 12th day of July, 2010, I called his home to check on him. He still remembers me and he always asks me where I am and how I'm doing. I told Johnny I'm in Vermont and feeling great. I told him I'm planning to go over to Montpelier tomorrow night and see my Fantasy Camp coach, former Red Sox pitcher Bill Monbouquette who's coming in with his team from Holyoke, Mass. Johnny asked me to say hello to Bill for him.

Unfortunately, Bill couldn't be there because of health problems. I obtained his phone number from his friend and called to wish him well. I reminded him how much fun I had at fantasy Camp in 1994. I let him know I had spoken to Johnny Pesky and to fellow Vermonter, Bill Lee. They both wish Bill the best of everything as he battles leukemia.

I enjoyed watching some of the game in Montpelier. I also enjoyed being interviewed by Vermont Public Television as part of a Ken Burns baseball special that will air on the 28th and 29th of September. My interview may not get off the cutting room floor but I look forward to seeing the program.

When I covered the Red Sox in 1991, one of the things I really looked forward to was seeing Johnny in full uniform, hitting fungo to infielders and outfielders. I would greet him and he would always ask me how things were going. One night, I let him know that the Red Sox had given me permission to be in the press box and the clubhouse after the game. I suspect that Johnny may have had quite a bit to do with that promotion from field level to a higher position. Johnny gave me a whack on the butt and said, "Way to go, Barn." I had made it to the major leagues.

One Sunday before a game with the Oakland A's, I was watching Johnny hit ground balls to Tyler Burleson, the son of former Red Sox shortstop, Rick, who was nicknamed "Rooster." Rick was serving as a hitting coach with the A's. I asked Johnny about Tyler.

"Tyler's ten years old, Barney. His dad was a great player here. I was talking to Rick about Tyler. Rick seemed to think his younger son, Chad, would be a better ballplayer, but the thing about Tyler is that he has no fear of the ball which is one of the prerequisites. I mean you have to have a certain amount of fear. Some people just run away from the plate. I'll give you an example. I remember when Jim Piersall was here. He first came up with the Red Sox in 1950. He was fiery, had incredible talent but also some severe psychological problems that caused him to black out and be hospitalized. He made a remarkable recovery and returned to Boston to play again from 1952 to 1958. A movie was made about Piersall's life called "Fear Strikes Out." With Tony Perkins playing Piersall and the late Karl Malden playing the dominating father.

Some guy would be a little wild on the mound. Jimmy would come to me and say, "John, you don't seem to budge at the plate."

"I said, if I throw a punch at your face, you're going to duck. You can see a thrown object. It's easy to get out of the way."

"Jimmy says," 'How do you avoid running away from the plate, moving back?'

"I told him, just put the bat on your shoulder and look that guy right in the eyes. Make it nice and level and go from there. Piersall was a pretty good player, a great outfielder and a pretty good hitter."

I remembered some of Jim Piersall's circus catches. He fell into the visitor's bullpen on one occasion. He had a rifle of a throwing arm and he made some incredible throws to home plate from right or center field.

As Johnny and I were talking, Mike Greenwell came strolling along the aisle behind us, on his way down to the clubhouse to get ready for the game with the Yankees. As previously mentioned, the game was a disaster with the Yankees winning 10 to 0. On Sunday, May 12th, the day Ted was honored, I had a chat in the dugout with Ed Linn, the creator of *Veeck, As In Wreck*, also author of *The Rivalry – Red Sox and Yankees*.

"Johnny, I told Ed Linn that when I met you in Winter Haven, I felt as if I had known you most of my life. We just had never met. You were busy on the field and I was in the stands with my dad."

Johnny laughed. "It all depends how you learn, Barn. Early in life, you learn from the people around you. We (Johnny and brother Vince) were fortunate to be able to hang around the ballpark in the summer and the hockey rink in the winter, up in Portland (Oregon.) We were never out on the streets looking for things to do. We had to work to get to the ballpark. We had to work to stay in the rink. The people in charge would more or less oversee what we were doing. That's what you responded to. We got kicked in the fanny once in a while. I had a great baseball coach so I was lucky. I've always had good luck with managers since I started playing ball. I played for a Hall of Famer my first year, right out of high school. His name was Heinie Manush (Manoosh). He was one of the best hitters in baseball from 1923 to 1939, hitting over .300 eleven times while playing for the Tigers, Braves, Senators, Pirates and Dodgers. He was inducted into the Hall in 1964. Then, I played for an outstanding person and a great minor league pitcher named Bill Birwell. When I came here, I played for Cronin, McCarthy, Boudreau and here I am."

Johnny looked pensive for a moment as he gazed out toward right field, perhaps thinking of his own days as a manager. "Your great players don't have any problems with management. Some guys can be a little drastic at times, like the late Casey Stengel for example. I thought he was great. Jimmy Dykes was great, although when I first came into the league, I had no love for Dykes. He was always on my case. I met Bob Kennedy during the war when he came up through Atlanta on a flight program. He was a third baseman for the White Sox and he played for Dykes.

"That blankety-blank Dykes, I said to Kennedy."

"Kennedy laughs. 'Oh, Johnny. He's great. The only reason he gets on you is because he likes you.' Well, that was good enough for me because I knew Bob pretty well. In those years, managers were different. I wouldn't say they were aloof but they were always with the press and the radio which was something that had to be done at the time. I think it's more glorified today because you have so much coverage. You're representing the ball club. A lot of times, things can be misinterpreted. That's understandable but sometimes you have to be very, very careful."

It was nearly 4 PM and it was time for Johnny to get ready for work. Some of the Yankee coaches were on the field. Big Frank Howard, a giant of a man, formerly of the Washington Senators, greeted Johnny from the other side of the screen. That was my cue to wrap what had been a wonderful visit with one of the true ambassadors of baseball. I thanked Johnny for his time, turned off the recorder, then just sat there soaking up the ambiance of Fenway and thinking about my good luck. I felt privileged to be there.

I was a little disappointed at the outcome of the game that night but that didn't keep me from being enthusiastic and excited about our story and the rest of the season. Joanne and I spent many warm summer evenings listening to the radio in our little backyard at 69 Victoria Street in Revere. One night, we were tuned in to Dale Arnold and Dan Shaughnessy together on a sports talk show on WEEI, which is presently the Red Sox flagship station. They were talking about Dan's book. Joanne decided to call the program and let them know it was all the negativity that was expressed every season by the fans and the media, most emphatically not the curse of Babe Ruth. Dan broke into good natured tears and said: "Joanne, you're right. It's all our fault." It was a hilarious radio moment in time and it just contributed to the fun we were having that delightful summer.

Eight

We had reached a point in the season and in our lives where it was time to make a major change in our lifestyle and our mode of transportation. We drove our little Dodge Colt back to California and traded with a man from Sebastopol for a 1976 Toyota pop-top camper. It was tiny but adequate for us and for Caspar. Now, we could travel and not have to pay for motels. While we were away from New England, the Red Sox went on a tear and were challenging the Yankees for first place until...

The Yankees came into Boston and all they did was sweep a four-game series. It was sickening and disgusting. So much for the challenge and so much for the season and all the optimism. The Minnesota Twins and the Atlanta Braves would end up playing in the 1991 World Series which was particularly noteworthy since both teams had finished in last place in 1990.

With about three weeks left in the season and the players just going through the motions since they were out of contention, I didn't have much of a reason to stay in the Boston area. However, one of the personal highlights of the season occurred when I was in the Red Sox clubhouse talking to Roger Clemens. I don't recall whether it was before or after a game but I had my recorder going and I asked Roger how he prepared for a game, mentally. He paused, held his chin in his hand, looked me straight in the eyes and said; "I prefer not to answer that question." Based on the current information we have on Roger's alleged use of steroids, I cannot help but wonder how he prepared for any game. I think it is sad that such a great player and such a fierce competitor may be denied entry into the Hall of Fame because he may have cheated.

In 1992, I returned to Winter Haven with Caspar as my traveling companion in the pop-top camper that would be home for a while. Joanne was staying in Santa Maria, California at her Uncle Walt's home. He was getting up in years, getting prepared for knee surgery and really enjoyed her company while I went off and wrote about baseball. Caspar would make himself comfortable in my lap and we would just drive for hundreds of miles at a leisurely pace. He was such a sweet loving pet. The Red Sox officials allowed me to park my camper right on the grounds at Chain-O-Lakes Park. How I loved those warm Florida evenings.

I greeted Johnny Pesky in almost the exact spot where we first met. He looked tanned, trim, and energetic.

"You're looking good, Mr. Pesky," I said.

"Well, I feel good, Barney."

Johnny was wearing his spring training uniform and was about to go outside. He was carrying a bat in his hands that had some light colored tape near the top that was badly discolored.

"What's the tape for, Johnny?" I wanted to know.

"That's bat control, Barney. The ball hits in the same place every time. When Ted hit .406, he had the same thing on his bat. When you don't have bat control, it's time to get out of the game."

I laughed. Pesky hadn't changed a bit. He was the same irrepressible story teller of the best damned stories in baseball, backed up by more than fifty years experience and knowledge of the game. Later that day, after the first exhibition game of the season, I was seated at a table with my good buddy, Joe Gildea, the press box steward in Winter Haven who always treated me very good whenever I needed anything in the press box. Johnny walked in and sat down at our table.

I turned on my little tape recorder. "Mind if we have a little session here, Johnny," I said. He laughed and just waved his hand in approval.

"Last year, you told me that Dykes used to get on your case. What did he say to you, Johnny?"

"I never played for him, Barney, but he used to call me some pretty bad names."

I laughed. "So Dykes was on your case if you went to Chicago or when the White Sox came to Fenway?"

"Oh yeah," Pesky said. "There was a lot of jockeying in those days. You could hear Dykes all over the park."

"Was it clean, Johnny?" I said.

Pesky grinned as he lit a cigar. "Man, it wasn't nice. Bench jockeys were more common in those days. You just didn't pay any attention to it. It just made you bear down more."

Johnny talked about managers. "I went to Detroit where Red Rolfe was fired and Fred Hutchinson took over. I spent two months in Washington with Bucky Harris. Joe McCarthy was probably the best manager I ever played for."

I asked Johnny to define the best.

"Well, there was something about him, his knowledge of the game and new people. He understood things I know I didn't understand. He was easy to talk to, very good, a fine man. Joe Gildea was puffing on his pipe and listening to our conversation.

"Who was it that kicked the catcher in the butt?" Joe said. "Was that McCarthy?"

"Yeah," Pesky answered. "McCarthy was supposed to have kicked Batts in the fanny. He told Mickey (McDermott) that he was kicking at the dirt. It was a play at the plate, funny as hell."

Our conversation shifted to Maurice (Mickey) McDermott who pitched for the Red Sox from 1948 to 1953 before going to the Washington Senators. I remembered collecting a lot of newspaper clippings about McDermott when I was a kid. I had turned a thick book of wallpaper samples into a sports scrapbook and I spent a lot of time clipping articles and putting them in the wallpaper book. I loved the cartoons by Bob Coyne of the old Boston Post.

McDermott was tall and very skinny but he had a blazing fastball and he made the Boston newspapers on a regular basis, sometimes on the society page. In *Summer of '49*, David Halberstam wrote about McDermott. "He did not try to be a flake. He *was* a flake. The Boston sportswriters were calling him 'Mickey' and he announced that he wanted to be called 'Lefty' because he thought and felt like a lefty. He sang at local nightclubs and told writers he would rather be a singer than a pitcher. Having been poor all his life, he loved to throw money around, now that he was making a big league salary, albeit a very small one."

"McDermott's financial status increased considerably as a result of Mrs. McDermott winning the lottery in Arizona a few years ago. I think it was six or seven million," Pesky told us.

"Maury's a rich man now. She gives him an allotment, a grand or two every month. Man, when they won, he called everybody in Boston. You knew when he called that he usually wanted something. Now, people want things from him."

I asked Johnny how tall McDermott was. "He was about 6'2", and I don't think he weighed more than 150 pounds when he first started pitching for us. Now he's fat and bald-headed."

"The names keep popping up from the past, Johnny. I'm thinking of Bob Kuzava."

"The white rat," Pesky said. "We used to call him the white rat."

"You came up with that, didn't you, Johnny?"

"No, I gave it to Whitey Herzog. I was on the ball club with him in Denver in the old American Association in 1955. I was Ralph Houk's coach. Gentleman, I've got to go home. Barney, I'll see you tomorrow." And with that, Johnny was out the door and another baseball bull session was history, another page or two for the book. I said goodnight to Joe Gildea. He asked me if I had talked to Sam Mele yet. Joe said Sam had some interesting stories about Ted Williams and that I should talk to him.

I enjoyed warm evenings beside the pool at the local Holiday Inn which was headquarters for players, fans, coaches and umpires. Nick's restaurant was next door, a very popular watering hole for lovers of good food and endless baseball discussions. It was one of those evenings by the pool when a Red Sox coach asked me if I had talked to Sam Mele. It was uncanny. I was meant to talk to him. A couple of days later, I caught up with Sam at the ballpark.

For the Meles, spring training was a family affair. I was introduced to Sam's lovely wife, Connie, their daughter Marilyn and their grandson Kyle. Sam and his wife were seated in a golf cart that Sam used to get around the training complex.

"I understand that Johnny Pesky introduced the two of you," I said to Sam. "Can you tell me about that?"

"Now, Barney," Sam says with a grin. "My wife is sitting right here and you expect me to tell you the story?" Sam laughed, saying he hadn't spoken to Pesky since that day in 1947, then said he was just pulling my leg.

"Connie was working at Jordan Marsh in Boston. Pesky had to go over there to sign some baseballs. He came back and told me he'd found a nice woman for me. I went over and met her. Now, here we are."

I complemented the two of them for being such a nice looking couple, then asked Sam about the stories having to do with Ted Williams' ribs. We arranged to meet and a couple of days later, Sam asked me to take a ride with him in his golf cart. He drove down a path to a position between two of the minor league fields where he could see what was going on and talk to me at the same time.

"Well, it was 1948 and we were coming back from St. Louis on the train. Ted had taken a liking to me ever since I joined the Red Sox in 1946. We liked to shadow box, you know, spar a little, so here we are in the middle aisle of the train. he throws his hands up and we begin sparring. Well, the next morning, Paul Schreiber, his roommate, says to me, 'What did you do to his ribs.?'"

"My answer is: 'What do you mean, what did I do?'

"Schreiber says, well he can't get out of bed. His ribs are bothering him."

"It happened that I had somehow separated a rib from a cartilage and Ted missed almost three weeks of the season. That was when we tied with Cleveland and they beat us in the playoffs. I'm sure, in those three weeks, he would have won 3, 4 or 5 games for us and we wouldn't have finished in a tie. If you were in the stands, you know what Boudreau and his boys did to us. It was just a freak accident. I was traded next June. I don't know if that incident had anything to do with it or not. Even up to this day, when I see Ted, he'll say; 'I remember you. You hurt my ribs.' Jokingly of course. I had torn up my ankle sliding into third base in St. Louis. I couldn't even walk, as a matter of fact. Cleveland took the train into Boston and they were having a gay time thinking it was more or less of a lost cause. They sure beat the heck out of us."

I asked Sam to tell me about his friendship with Ted Williams.

"It all started when I was in college. My coach was the late Bill McCartney of NYU. He was very friendly with the Boston organization. He used to drive up to Boston on weekends and I'd work out with the Red Sox. I'll never forget. One day, I'm taking batting practice and I took a pitch. This voice behind home plate says; 'Why did you take that pitch?'"

"I thought the ball was outside, I say to the voice."

"The voice says; 'It was, but it was high enough for a strike.'"

"When I walk out of the batting cage, he calls me over and it was Ted Williams. Of course, I had heard so much about him. I was in awe of the guy. From that day on, he took a liking to me. He used to call me up to warm up with him, then I'd sit with him on the bus. He'd talk hitting, hitting, hitting! Whenever you got off the bus, you felt like you were the greatest hitter in the world. He made you believe in yourself and of course, you had to listen because he was such a great hitter and an equally great teacher."

I recalled some of the legendary exploits of the giant of a Red Sox player. "I heard he had awesome vision, Sam. When I was growing up, I remember hearing that he could tell if a pitch was a fraction of an inch outside the strike zone. The umpires would be hesitant to call a strike on him because they knew he could tell."

"I heard the same thing," Sam replied. "What was amazing with Ted was that he could pick up the spin of the ball twenty feet away, how it was going to break, and he was a great student of pitchers. If he didn't know a pitcher, he'd go up and down the bench. I remember being in the old Eastern League and a couple of pitchers had come up to the big leagues from there. Ted didn't know them and he came right over to me and said; 'Do you know these guys? What do they throw? What do they like to throw. How does their ball move?'"

"Up and down the bench he would go, asking questions. If he didn't know the pitcher, he wanted to learn everything about him, and of course, he was such a great hitter that he could take two strikes and see how the guy reacted."

I laughed. "And if somebody did get him out, Sam, he probably knew what the pitch was and they wouldn't get him out with it a second time."

Sam grinned. "I remember Bobby Doerr, Ted, Dom DiMaggio, Pesky and myself would all sit in a group and talk about what had happened during the game, not only to us, but all the guys. That was one thing Ted always told me. He'd say; 'You get in front of your locker after the game and you say to yourself: How did we make out? How did I do? Did I do anything to help cause our winning or losing the game?' Winning always came first with Ted. If I got into a slump, I'd go right to him. He'd tell me exactly what I was doing. 'You're pulling your head off the ball', he'd say, 'If you're in a slump, try and drive the ball through the box.'"

"It was great advice," Sam said, "coming from a guy that hit .406 in 1941. That particular instruction made you watch the ball more closely and longer. It didn't make any difference if you pulled the ball as long as you made solid contact."

"What a great teacher you had," I said to Sam, recalling that he was Rookie of The Year in 1947, hitting .302 with 12 home runs and 75 runs batted in.

"Absolutely," said Sam. "I don't know if you ever read his book called *The Science of Hitting*. It's one of the best books ever written on hitting a baseball."

I told Sam about being at Fenway Park in 1991 on the day they honored Ted for hitting .406. He had been in the clubhouse on Saturday, visiting with Wade Boggs when he reminded Boggs of a pitch he had taken ten days earlier against the Yankees. Boggs was flabbergasted that Williams had such total recall of individual pitches. Sam talked about Ted's amazing memory.

"To this day, he can tell you about certain pitchers, how they got him out, and he recalls specific games. That's how thorough he was about the game, especially about hitting and you know, there's one thing people forget. Ted did not have a lot of speed, as people knew. If he did, he'd hit .390 or .400 damned near every year if he could run, but that's another thing. They forget he was a pretty darned good outfielder, especially in Fenway Park. Nobody could play the wall the way Ted did. Yastrzemski came very close, probably as an equal to Ted, playing that left field wall. Ted had sure hands, absolute sure hands. Maybe his range wasn't all that great because he didn't have great speed but absolutely sure hands. I'll bet he would have made a great first baseman, too."

"He certainly had the height," I said to Sam. "That would have been a good transition for him."

"Let me tell you. I was traded to Washington and I heard some talk from opposing teams first basemen. When they were holding runners on and Williams was batting, they were scared! I know it's true because when I went to Washington, Mickey Vernon hurt his ankle and Bucky Harris, the manager, said; 'Can anyone play first base?' I played there a little in the service, so I played first and Boston happened to be coming to town. I'm playing first and Dom DiMaggio gets a hit, so I'm holding him on, looking right down Williams' throat, the barrel of the bat." Sam's voice rose as he recalled the moment. "I'm telling you. I don't know how close it was, but it seemed like it was about twenty yards away and if he had ever pulled one down the line, I don't know what the heck I would have done. Fortunately for me, he got the ball in the air and hit it through the box, but it was very fearful, really."

The casual conversation with Sam Mele was filled with Ted Williams stories and that was fine with me. Any story about my hero made for enjoyable listening and I knew the potential readers of the story would enjoy reading about them. The stories gave me more of an insight into Ted's private life. He was a proud man and he was fiercely loyal to his friends. If you were a friend of Ted Williams, you were a very fortunate person because the "Splendid Splinter" (Ted's nickname) chose his friends carefully. The adulation and respect between Ted and Sam was crystal clear. There was a gleam in Sam's eyes as if he was reliving every moment he could recall.

Like Sam, I couldn't help but wonder at the impact Ted's rib injury ad on that 1948 season. Like so many other bizarre incidents confounding the efforts of the Red Sox to get to a World Series and win, the story fit right into the niche. By virtue of telling what happened, Sam was willing to take the blame for the unfortunate and untimely injury. Sixty-two years later that doggone playoff game is still vivid.

It's much more fun to replay Game 6 of the 1975 World Series, arguably one of the greatest World Series games ever played. I was in Saudi Arabia, where I was employed by Lockheed Aircraft International and I was listening to the game on shortwave radio. It kept fading in and out. It was seven-thirty in the morning and I was supposed to go to work. I called in sick that day. I would not take my ear away from the radio. I could visualize what was happening on the field when Bernie Carob hit the pinch hit home run and then Carlton Fisk, a Vermont guy, hit the home run that won the game as he danced around the bases, urging the baseball to stay in fair territory. Nice going, Pudge. People spilled out into the streets of Boston. It was only Game Six. The Reds won the Series the next day. How bizarre!

Were the baseball gods just playing cruel jokes on this team? If so, there were more to come three years later when Bucky 'f-----g' Dent hit the pop fly over the left field wall and stole a victory. Another cruel joke! Was somebody laughing somewhere when that miserable hit broke the hearts of millions of New Englanders? There was more to come when the champagne was on ice at Shea Stadium and the Red Sox were ready to celebrate. Oops! The ground ball went right through Bill Buckner! Can you believe it? Where were you when it happened? I remember exactly where I was, watching the game at a place called "The Cellar" which was actually upstairs in a restaurant in the picturesque little village of Mendocino, California. It ruined my whole evening.

Time was running short for questions. I knew that Sam disliked long interviews and I had already taken up about an hour and a half of his time. I shifted the focus to Sam's career as a player and a manager.

"I went to Washington in '49. I was there in 1950 and '51, then I was traded to the Chicago White Sox. I played for one heck of a manager in Paul Richards, an absolute 'fundamentalist.' In baseball parlance, fundamentals means working on little things that advance runners and often win games. A sacrifice generally occurs when there is a runner on first base and the manager wants to get him to second where he will be in scoring position. The batter essentially gives himself up by bunting the ball. The throw will go to first as the runner advances. Sounds easy. Things don't always work out that way. If there are two strikes on a batter, and he bunts the ball foul, he is automatically out. A well placed bunt is fun to watch. If the batter bunts and pops the ball up, it could turn into a double play.

"Other fundamentals include 'hit and run.' Again, let's suppose there is a runner on first and the objective is to advance him to second or third, so on a prearranged signal from the dugout, like the manager going through a bunch of motions then pulling on his right ear lobe, the runner knows to go when the batter swings. If the batter swings and misses, the play is blown. If he lines a hit to the outfield, the strategy has worked well. The, there is the 'sacrifice fly.' If there are less than two outs and there is a runner on third, that runner can tag up and score on a long fly ball. The batter gets credit for a run batted in, so again, it's good strategy. Of course, it's much better if the batter hits the ball out of the ballpark and two runs score. When a team is well-versed in fundamentals, chances are they will be successful over the course of an entire season."

Sam continued. "We didn't always have the greatest of ball clubs with the White Sox but we were always finishing second to the Yankees because of Richards. He made us practice fundamentals after games and before games that helped us to win."

I asked Sam if he was there when the White Sox started developing the "Go-Go" guys like Orestes "Minnie" Minoso and "Jungle" Jim

Rivera.

"I was there. I played the outfield with Rivera and Minoso." Exactly. Sam's voice was rising. He was excited as he recalled the days of playing with two of the fastest men in baseball. The White Sox were fun to watch.

Sam continued. "Chico Carasquel was at short and Nellie Fox was the second baseman. Pretty good club. The pitching staff was pretty good but again, it was the fundamentals that carried us to second place. The White Sox traded me to St. Louis for Johnny Groth. That was the winter of 1954 when the Browns moved to Baltimore and became the Orioles. I played there a year and a half then went back over to the Red Sox."

I asked Sam about his relationship with Tom Yawkey.

"You know, I don't know how they got me back but I had known Mr. Yawkey for years, ever since signing my first contract in New York at the hotel where he was staying. I'd see him in the winter time and we struck up a good relationship. Later on when I was managing in Minnesota, I'd call him or he'd call me. He'd always say; 'If anything happens in Minnesota, you call me and you will have a job with me.' Well, it happened in 1967 that I was fired. I called Mr. Yawkey, came up to his office and he said; 'You've got a job here.' He never forgot. I've been with the organization ever since."

"I was very loyal to the Red Sox, Barney. As a matter of fact, and it may sound like a lot of bull but when I managed Minnesota and we beat Boston, I felt a little bad about it. Whenever we weren't playing at Fenway, I was rooting like a son-of-a-gun for them, for Mr. and Mrs. Yawkey and Dick O'Connell, their general manager, a great friend of mine. They were excellent people.

"In '67, Calvin Griffith called me into his office in Minnesota and said he was going to make a change. He offered me a job. He says; 'Listen, you're with me. You want a job. You've got it.' But, I knew Mr. Yawkey promised me one and naturally, I'd be a lot closer to home, so I accepted Mr. Yawkey's job over the one with the Twins. I had a real good ball club, a well-knit family ball club in Minnesota. We started running and won a pennant in '65. In '66, we finished second, then I got canned in '67, so here we are."

1967 was a magical year for the Red Sox. Under the tutelage of Dick Williams, a fiery young manager, they defeated the Minnesota Twins on the last day of the regular season and won the right to play the Cardinals in the World Series. For once, things seemed to be going right for the Red Sox, but on a hot night in August, things went tragically wrong for Tony Conigliaro, a Revere boy and a local hero. Tony C. had it all, good looks and a powerful swing. A Jack Hamilton fast ball smashed into his face. It was a terrifying moment. I was listening to the game on a Hartford, Connecticut radio station, WTIC, at McGuire AFB, New Jersey where I was stationed. The sound of the ball striking Tony C's head reverberated throughout the ballpark with a sickening thud. Number 25 was down for the count. No matter what happened for the rest of the season, a pall of gloom was cast over the clubhouse. A few years later, Tony would suffer a devastating heart attack where his brain was without oxygen for more than four minutes. For the rest of his young life, he was confined to bed in a rest home. He died at the age of 45 but left a lasting legacy.

I brought myself back to the moment in the golf cart and focused on wrapping up the interview with Sam. "Here we are in 1992 and all of a sudden, twenty five years have flown by. It's a different feeling here in Winter Haven, isn't it, Sam?"

"Well, yeah, it's different for a number of reasons. We're going to move. I don't know anything about why or whatever. That's none of my business, but there's a different feeling here because each year, we get better and better prospects plus new coaches and instructors. They not only want to develop ballplayers. They are instilling winning attitudes and that makes it great for the entire organization, from the top, right on down, for Eddie Kenney Sr. and his son. There's a lot of emphasis on fundamentals here. There's that word again. By the time a player gets to the big leagues, he's prepared, because he's learned good fundamental baseball here."

Sam Mele was making timeout signals with his hands. That told me it was time to wrap things up. Sam had told me some fascinating stories that gave me a real insight into the life of a man who was a player, a coach and a manager. What a student of the game. Sam learned well from his early mentor, Ted Williams. It must have been a heck of a punch that caused Ted's rib injury, I thought to myself. Certainly, it was unfortunate and unintentional. And how many opposing managers feel bad when they beat the Red Sox?

Today, Sam Mele is living in Quincy, Mass. with his lovely wife, Connie. He's had some medical problems but his mind is sharp and he and I have enjoyed some great conversations. I've also learned that the Red Sox chose not to give Sam a World Series ring. He worked for them for over 40 years. I personally believe he deserves a ring.

Caspar, our very intelligent and beautiful Lynxpoint Siamese.

The author, posing at City of Palms Park in Ft. Myers at Red Sox Fantasy camp in 1994.

EJ and the late Dick Radatz, 1994.

The late Joanne Barney, loving Vermont ice cream.

Joanne in Vermont.

EJ and Red Sox Legend Bobby Doerr

EJ and his roommate at Red Sox Fantasy Camp, 1994.

EJ with the late Ken Coleman, 1994.

Sketch by George Guzzi.

Jerry Remy & Johnny Pesky with a friend in Winter Haven, 1992.

Team photo at Red Sox Fantasy camp in 1994. EJ in middle back row. Our coaches, Bill Monboquette on left and Frank Malzone on right.

Sketch by George Guzzi, for David Halberstam's book; Teammates.

Ted Williams tips his cap at Fenway, May 1991.

Johnny Pesky, flanked by two pals; 1992 in Winter Haven.

Wade Boggs in Winter Haven, 1992.

Nine

Joanne was with her uncle in Santa Maria, California and it was getting close to Easter Sunday. I wanted to get back to her as soon as possible. I felt a sense of urgency but was unable to figure it out. At any rate, Caspar and I headed the pop-top toward California. I recall stopping at a rest stop in Georgia and letting him out. I ended up having to chase him through some brush and I got a little winded. I also felt some mild chest pain but didn't think too much of it.

While Caspar and I were in Winter Haven, he performed a most amazing feat, just for me. It was a beautiful Florida evening and he and I were hanging out at one of the baseball fields. We were the only ones around and there was enough light so I could see what he was doing. He took off running as fast as his legs would carry him, toward the outfield where he ran from right field to left field, then back toward third base and around the infield, tagging all the bases. I watched in amazement as he ran to the pitcher's mound then to home plate. He ran through both dugouts and the coaching boxes then he came back and sat in front of me as if to say: "See what I just did." He knew about baseball and when he was less than a year old, he knew how to get out of a tent that we were sleeping in at a U.S. Navy recreation area in Maine. It was raining lightly and I told Joanne I wanted to keep him inside. We closed our eyes and had just started to drift off when I heard a zipper being unzipped, then another one. Our very intelligent cat had just used his teeth and his paws to let himself outside. We were very impressed.

The rest of our return trip to California was uneventful. I didn't have any more chest pain and the little Toyota purred right along. Joanne and her uncle were happy to see me. Walt was fun to be around. He had lots of stories to tell and he just allowed us to relax and enjoy his modest home. He loved Caspar as well. One evening, the three of us went out to a movie. We left the back door to the house open so Caspar could come and go as he pleased. When we returned, there was no sign of him. The weather was terrible. A severe thunderstorm was passing through the area and there were high winds. When he didn't show up the next day, we began to get worried. We started looking everywhere, in alley ways, behind a nearby shopping mall, across the busy highway in a large park and at the local vet's offices.

There was no sign of him. By the fourth day, we were disconsolate. We had no idea what to do next. I saw a group of neighborhood boys playing outside the house. I went out and asked them if anyone had seen a white Siamese cat. One of the boys said he saw a cat that matched the description on a roof a few blocks away. He went to see if the cat was still there. About a half hour later, there was a knock on the door. When Joanne opened it, a boy handed Caspar to her. She cried tears of joy. I was thrilled. He looked a little thinner and his eyelids were partially closed, but otherwise, he was fine. We wanted to give the boys reward money but the parents would have none of that so we bought them about $50 worth of ice cream and pizza, then invited about five boys in to have a feast. They loved it. Caspar had been totally spooked by the thunderstorm and just decided to hang out beneath the edge of an overhang up on the roof of a house, until he was rescued. He was safe and warm and we kept him in close proximity to us the rest of the time we were in Santa Maria.

We left Walt's place a few days later and drove north to Leo and Marlene's house in Petaluma, Joanne's hometown. I was taking a refreshing shower when I felt some numbness in my left wrist. I dismissed it as a temporary glitch and continued with my shower. A couple of days later, on a Wednesday morning to be exact, Joanne asked if the numbness was still there. My answer was yes and she insisted that we proceed to the David Grant Medical Center at Travis Air Force Base in Fairfield, California. We checked into the emergency room where I was given some routine tests, including having pins stuck in my right and left wrists. I couldn't feel the pin on the left wrist. They performed an EKG and a couple of hours later, a second EKG. The results baffled the doctors. They were getting different readings on each one of the procedures. Things did not add up, so I was admitted for a heart catherization the following morning. It was my first heart catherization and it was a painless procedure. What doctors saw on the screen alarmed them. They calmly informed me that I would be taken in an ambulance to Mercy General Hospital in Sacramento for an angioplasty. I was told that it too was a painless procedure and that Walter Matthau had even made a movie about his experiences.

Everything sounded fairly easy and straightforward. Joanne and Caspar followed the ambulance.

Upon arrival at the hospital, I was quickly offloaded and wheeled into the cath lab where the procedure would take place. I was draped and prepared but something didn't seem right. After some discussions among the team of doctors, I was wheeled out of the lab and on to an elevator where Joanne met us, wondering how they finished so fast. She was told that nothing had been done and the doctor wanted to see us in my room. What was going on, we wondered? We were about to find out.

A cardiologist met us in the room and explained that there was so much plaque buildup in the arteries that an angioplasty was out of the question. Surgery would be required, in the form of a bypass, a five way bypass. One artery was 99% blocked. Another was 97% blocked. Without immediate intervention, I was headed for a massive heart attack. I'll never forget what the doctor said to us.

"Mr. Barney, when you have a rattlesnake in your pocket, you want to get it out as quickly as possible." They also told me that I had a very strong heart and my chances of survival were excellent. I had no time to think about the odds. Surgery was scheduled for the following morning. I would be the first patient in the operating room. Mercy

General Hospital was renowned for the high quality of their bypass procedures as well as the patient survival rates. I was in the right place at precisely the right time. I'm sure they gave me some relaxation medication the night before. I had no apprehension whatsoever. I did have visions of seeing the operating room doors swing open. The only thing I saw was the back of my eyelids. I was "under" for a little over six hours. My breastbone was sawed open and I was placed on a heart-lung breathing machine while the very skilled surgeons performed the bypass. The only word I could think of was "miraculous."

When they woke me up in the recovery room, I was delighted to see Joanne, my stepdaughter, Marlene and my stepdaughter, Kim. They were happy to see me open my eyes. I was happy to open them. I looked pretty scary. There were tubes sticking out of my stomach and I had other stuff attached to me. My chest felt stiff but there was no pain from the surgery. They gave me a "huggie" pillow to use in the event of a sneeze. There was really no way my chest would come apart but the pillow was comforting. I spent seven days in the hospital and did not require any pain pills. That was a good sign.

Joanne had made up a comfortable bed inside the camper and it looked so nice. Caspar was happy to see me and I was happy to see him. From the time we started in the emergency room at Travis, up to the time I was discharged was very stressful for Joanne. At one point, she went to the little chapel room in the hospital and during a silent prayer, she felt a warm hand on her shoulder. I felt that my higher power was with me from the beginning, guiding the surgeons through the delicate operation.

A few years ago, my dear friend, Alex Randall of the Virgin Islands, did a computer printout of my astrological chart. What came out was a perfect double trine. Each of my aspects were exactly 60 degrees apart. When lines were drawn, they formed two triangles, one inverted. Alex told Joanne she should stay close to me because it appeared that I am a very lucky man. All of the planets in the universe were in perfect alignment at 12:30 am., Eastern time, on the morning of February 17th, 1937.

I am a great believer in the importance of numbers and the place they have in our lives. Numerology is the science of numbers and the numbers often have great meaning. To illustrate my point, I recall going to the horse races in Salem, New Hampshire in 1963, just prior to traveling to a new Air Force assignment in the Azores. I looked at the racing charts the night before and I decided to use my dad's home phone number in the twin daily double which consisted of four races, the first and second and as I recall, the seventh and eighth races. The digits in the phone number were 2597. The next day, I made a $2 wager, using those numbers. The two horse and the five horse won the first two races. I had an option to change the last two choices but decided to stick with them. After the 9 horse won the seventh race, I went upstairs to the betting windows and asked how much I would win if the 7 horse came through. The answer was $18,000. The man also advised me to keep my tickets because if the 1 horse won the 8th race, I would win the consolation prize. I wanted to know how much that would be and I learned that it would be about $2500. My brother Bob and I were hanging on the rail for the 8th race. The horses came thundering across the finish line and I saw that the 7 horse was way back in the pack. At first, I was disappointed, then I looked at the tote board and saw that the number 1 horse had finished first. We ran upstairs toward the betting windows. I was a winner! A man told me to slow down, so the IRS people wouldn't see me. We were approached by a 10% man, a person who cashes the ticket for ten percent of the gross value. I would have to give him the winning ticket. My brother had a fit. "You gave him your ticket. What if he doesn't come back?" I told Bob not to worry. I knew the guy would be back. Otherwise, he might find himself floating in a nearby river with cement tied to him.

Sure enough, the man came back and advised me that he had to go and get the cash and when he returned, I was to follow him into the men's room where he would hand me the money, then I would duck into a stall and count it. if I was satisfied, that would be the end of the transaction. He came back and I did exactly as he instructed. He handed me a "wad" of hundred dollar bills. There were 23 of them and I was a very happy man. I thanked the guy and my brother and I headed for his residence, a nearby mobile home. I gave my brother a hundred dollar bill. When we got to his place, we went inside and his wife wanted to know how we made out. I said we didn't do very well, then I took the hundred dollar bills out and spread them all over the kitchen table. We enjoyed celebrating the windfall and I never bet on horses again. My only regret is that I didn't make a bigger wager. If I was so sure of those numbers, perhaps I should have bet $100 instead of $2.

Joanne drove the camper to the home of Joel and Carol Clark in Sacramento. They graciously opened their home and their hearts to us for as long as we needed them. Thanks guys. They are both very special and always will be.

Most of my six month recovery time was spent either at Leo and Marlene's home in Petaluma or at Shirley Hunt's home in Belle Marin Keys, in Marin County. Shirley is the current president of PSI World. Her home was quiet and peaceful and very restful for me. I was soon walking every day and getting my right leg to work well again. The doctors had taken a vein out of my right leg to make the five new arteries. Consequently, the leg was stiff and sore and it took a lot of walking and exercises to bring it back to normal My chest felt very stiff and I was afraid to let anyone touch it, even Joanne. She felt she was trying to comfort me and I was pulling away from her. Today, eighteen years after the bypass, I am very comfortable. I am feeling good. Three of the five arteries got plugged up again, but the two main arteries are functioning well. I am thriving on the good clean air and the low altitude here in Vermont.

Sometime in 1992, we went to Oregon to visit Joanne's daughter, Lori and her family. While there, we traded in the pop-top for a Toyota Dolphin mini Motor home. We had to climb up into the over-head bed and I had to bow my head a little so I wouldn't hit the ceiling but it was definitely a step up for us as we re-assumed the role of just being vagabonds. We were both retired, Joanne from 25 years of teaching in California and myself with a USAF retirement plus my full social security check coming in every month. There was always enough for whatever we chose to be doing. By January, 1993, my recovery was going very well and I had Red Sox fever. I wanted to go to Ft. Myers and see the new digs for the team.

Dave and Roberta and the children were living on base in Rio Vista, California at the U.S. Coast Guard station. We parked the motor home outside and spent a lot of time with them. Joanne thought it would be nice if Roberta and 4-year-old Jenna came with us to Florida. I had visions of selling my beautiful Ted Williams photos. We had already decided to put the photo on redwood and have it laminated. All we had to do was find a way to mass produce the product and we would sell dozens of them. Wishful thinking? Probably.

In Florida, we put a nice brass plaque under the photo that read: "I tip my hat to the fans." Under that in block letters was: TED WILLIAMS - 1991.

Ultimately, we met a guy in Ft. Myers that passed himself off as a promoter and a man of action who clipped sports pages, then distributed them to men's restrooms in restaurants and sports bars all over the Ft. Myers area, the spring training home of the Red Sox and the Minnesota Twins. It was a lot different scene than laid back Winter Haven. We started mass producing the redwood plaques in the living room of this guy's house. We had the motor home parked in the yard for sleeping quarters and we were having a rollicking good time. I recall having a few drinks of something one Saturday night and feeling pretty tipsy. I wasn't getting much work done on the photos. The guy was a bit flaky and unreliable and we just didn't care for the drug and alcohol environment so we terminated the project and without saying goodbye to our "friend," we left the house and took the motor home to the parking lot of the Holiday Inn. The four of us were living in the Dolphin which meant very close quarters. I will never forget the very windy night when there was a hurricane in the weather forecast. I enjoyed having a few drinks in the lounge and meeting some of the Red Sox personnel, including Lee Stange and the late Felix Maldonado. It was close to 11 pm. when I called it a night and went to the motor home. The wind velocity was increasing. It was howling and the rain was coming down. We were rocking and rolling and praying we wouldn't get blown down the road. Later, we learned that the winds reached speeds up to 100 mph and a considerable amount of damage was done to Florida's east coast.

I was in a bad mood much of the time. I was smoking whenever I could sneak one and I was feeling very insecure about the bypass that had given me a new start for my life. I was plugging up the new arteries with the nicotine habit. What should have been a joyous time in my life turned into a not so good time that finally caused Joanne, Robert and Jenna to leave me and return to California. They just couldn't stand being around me and putting up with my foul moods. There are two major emotions in life, love and fear. Man, I was clinging to the fear, the kind one associates with dying rather than living and cramming all the love that's possible into every moment.

After the girls left me, I roamed around Florida with the motor home, spending some time back in Winter Haven where the Cleveland Indians had opened their 1993 spring training camp for the first time. I stopped by the Holiday Inn to have a beer and enjoy some baseball conversations. I had several copies of my Ted Williams photo and I was very proud of them. I was talking to a man named Alan Weiss from Miami. He liked my photo and he suggested I show it to the gentleman on the other side of the circular bar. Alan told me the man's name was John Savage and he was one of the co-owners of Red Sox Fantasy Camp. I finished my beer, thanked Mr. Weiss, then went over and introduced myself to Mr. Savage. When I showed him the photo, he said; "For 200 of those, I'll give you fantasy camp." We shook hands and I planted the statement in my brain for later recall.

I sold a few copies of Ted Williams on redwood for $50 each, one to Tony Fossas, a Red Sox relief pitcher with an inspirational story to tell, one to Mike Greenwell's brother at their batting cage facility in Ft. Myers and one to a sports bar in exchange for $50 worth of food and drinks. The rest of that year is blurry. I drove the motor home north to the Boston area and parked it at the Hanscom Air Force Base 'Fam Camp'. 'Fam Camp' is a term for "Family Campground." It's near the base and it's an area that has hookups for motor homes, and of course, there are hot showers available. It was okay but the New

England weather was cold and miserable and I was the same as the weather. I watched the Red Sox lose to Cleveland on opening day on television, then decided to return to California, specifically to northern California where we parked our motor home on Nog Johnson's property. He was a sweet man who allowed us to park on his wooded property free of charge. The huge front door of his very rustic old house was always unlocked, so we had access to his phone and to the restroom. Nog was involved with building a replica of a California Grey Whale. It would be on wheels! Imagine a 40 ft. grey whale being driven around town. It was a sight to behold and we helped him realize his dream. In November, 1993, I called John Savage and reminded him of our conversation. We closed the deal over the phone. he would buy 200 Ted Williams photos at fifteen dollars apiece for a total of $3,000. That plus $500 would pay for the cost of fantasy camp. I remember getting another call a couple of days later at which time they asked me if I would take the Twins' fantasy camp. My answer was a very firm "no." It was Red Sox or nothing. I was told I would receive confirmation in the mail. The camp would take place in January at the brand new training facility in Ft. Myers. I had a couple of months to get my body in shape for baseball. I was just shy of my 57th birthday and about a year and a half past the five way bypass, the miracle that saved my life. The extraordinary vision I had always harbored in my mind, that of being involved with the Boston Red Sox, was about to come true. I would wear the uniform.

Ten

Have you ever dreamed of being a major league baseball player? Have you ever found yourself wondering what it would feel like to be a member of the Boston Red Sox? Have you ever had the feeling you were out there on the field and playing in front of a sellout crowd? I was told that all those feelings and more would happen at Red Sox Fantasy Camp.

It was early January and all I had to do was figure out a way to get to Florida without spending a lot of money. The United States Navy helped me travel from Alameda Naval Air Station in the Bay Area to Lemoore Naval Air Station, near Fresno. After an overnight stay, I would fly in a Navy P3 aircraft from Lemoore to Jacksonville Naval Air Station in Florida. The aircraft commander regaled us with personal accounts of landing on an aircraft carrier as it was pitching and rolling. He likened it to landing on a postage stamp that never stopped moving. I gained new respect for the brave Navy pilots that were required to perform those duties every day without a malfunction.

The six and a half hour flight to Jacksonville was smooth and uneventful. I was the only passenger and I enjoyed talking to the flight crew members and telling them about my baseball exploits and of course, the Ted Williams photo. If they were not already Red Sox fans, they were when I got through telling them all about the team.

When I disembarked from the aircraft in Jacksonville, I couldn't believe how cold I felt. The temperature was in the thirties, just a little above freezing. The citrus crops were in danger. I made a reservation with Amtrak the next day and one day later, I was on the way to Ft. Myers. The second leg of the trip involved taking a bus from Ft. Lauderdale over to Ft. Myers where I would have lodging at the Sheraton Hotel. Everything I needed was at the front desk when I checked in, including my very own, brand new, authentic Red Sox uniform.

As soon as I got in the room, I tried on the uniform, then stood in front of a full length mirror and admired what I saw. I was a little too old to be an active player, but I felt as if I was twenty years younger and the uniform looked awesome! I had asked for and received number 17, my birth date and what I considered to be my lucky number. The uniform was a perfect fit. Later that evening, my "roomie" arrived from Rhode Island. His name was Judd Hurd. His son, Chris, was also at camp. They were both great gentlemen. Judd was a super roommate. He was just as excited as I was about being there. The next day, Sunday, we went out to the training facility, dressed in full uniform, traveling on a team bus. We would get checked in, be assigned locker space and meet some of the pros that were in camp.

If you're a Red Sox fan, you may recognize some of these names from the past. They included Gary Allenson, Gary Bell, Bernie Carbo, Denny Doyle, Bobby Doerr, Walt Dropo, Mike Easier, Russ Gibson, Rich Gale, the late Mark Fidrych, Ferguson Jenkins, Dalton Jones, Bill "Spaceman" Lee, Rick Miller, Frank Malzone, Bill Monbouquette, Jerry Moses, the late Dick Radatz, Jose' Santiago, Lee Stange, Marc Sullivan and Rick Wise.

There were nine teams and two pro managers for each team. The pros got together and picked their team members. My coaches were Frank Malzone and Bill Monbouquette, two great Red Sox players from the sixties. Sadly, Mark Fidrych and Dick Radatz are no longer with us. Radatz died from injuries suffered in a fall down a flight of stairs in his home. Mark was killed in a tragic accident on his farm in Massachusetts. He was working underneath a farm vehicle that was running and somehow, his shirt collar got caught up in the rotating flywheel and strangled him. I have a nice photo of Dick Radatz and me sitting in a dugout. He has his arm over my shoulder. He was fun to be around as was Mark.

Bill "Spaceman" Lee lives here in Vermont, over in Craftsbury, about thirty miles or so from East Burke where I'm located. He is a very busy man, constantly in demand for various events around New England, at Fenway Park and other places. Before the leaves turn, I plan to find a way to have a face to face meeting with him. This is just another reason why I am in exactly the right place to finish this story, here in the heart of Red Sox nation where the enthusiasm for the team is absolutely contagious.

On that first Sunday at camp, we tossed baseballs around and played in a very informal scrimmage game. I was getting ready to hit against Bob Stanley when I heard a voice behind me say: "Hey, number 17, grab a bat." The voice belonged to Ferguson Jenkins, a Hall of Fame pitcher. "Fergie" had me throw a glove on the ground to use as a plate, then he told me how he wanted me to prepare to hit.

"Cock that bat," he said. "I don't want to see it resting on your shoulder. Be ready to take a good level swing at the pitch. Be ready to hit." It was great advice coming from one of the great pitchers in the game. Ferguson Jenkins racked up 284 career victories, won a National League Cy Young award in 1971 and made it on to two All Star teams during his career.

I stepped into the batters' box and followed his advice by hitting a ground ball to the left of the mound. I was an easy out but later that night in a hotel elevator, Bob Stanley said; "Jeez, Barney, you almost took my leg off with that shot." That was the tone of fantasy camp, pure fun and the thrill of getting lessons from some of the best players ever to play the game.

We had our own locker spaces in the sparkling new clubhouse. My name was over my locker space and each day, there would be my freshly laundered uniform hanging in the locker, just like the major leagues. Gary Allenson's locker was next to mine. Gary was on the miracle team of 1967 and he was a wonderful locker mate, always smiling and offering tidbits of good advice for making every moment in camp a little more fun if that was possible. Bill Lee and Denny Doyle would lead the morning "limbering up" sessions when they would tell us that this would be as good as we would feel all day. After warm ups, we would break off to our respective teams and play intramural games. I was not a very good outfielder. In retrospect, I should have signed on as a first baseman, my favorite position.

Baseball players love to play pranks on teammates and I recall that one day, I was sent to the clubhouse to get a box of right-handed curve balls. Of course, I knew that was a big joke on me. When I returned empty handed, I said they were all out of that type of baseball. It reminded me of my twenty year Air Force career when an airman would be told to find a bucket of "prop wash" or a coil of "flight line." Funny stuff. I laugh right now as I think about it.

At lunch time, we would all gather under a large tent where a buffet lunch would be served, lots of potato salad, chicken and ham. Red Sox players would always be there to talk about their baseball careers and answer questions from the campers. Bobby Doerr was a very popular guest. I am so very proud of the photo of us together on the front of this book. I felt a special kinship with Bobby, having previously met him in 1991.

Evenings at the Sheraton Hotel were awesome. Everyone would gather downstairs for dinner and then entertainment put on by the co-emcees, Gary Bell, Dick Radatz and Bill Monbouquette who still remembers getting "goosed" by his colleagues. It was hilarious. Poor Bill. The three men cracked us up with their antics. Awards were given out to campers for sensational plays or for something totally absurd like dropping an easy fly ball or tripping over a base.

Joe Castiglione, the long time voice of the Red Sox, was attending his second fantasy camp and called it "the only place outside Disney World where people wear a constant smile for a week." When I was asked to give a quote that would appear in the program guide, I said: "For a man to fulfill every one of his boyhood dreams is a privilege reserved for Greek Gods. I am profoundly grateful to be here."

Every day at camp was awesome, starting with breakfast at the

Sheraton. We were encouraged to share tables with the pros and join in the conversations. I don't recall who I sat with but I do remember that there were always stories about baseball or golf. Ballplayers love to tell stories about their golf exploits. Most of them are avid golfers because golf, like baseball, requires swinging a club at a round object. The advantage of golf is that the object is in a stationary position. The disadvantage is that one must keep his or her head down in order to strike the object. Which is more difficult, hitting a 95 mph fastball or driving a golf ball straight down the fair- way for 250 yards or more?

One afternoon after a game against the campers from the Minnesota Twins, I was outside the clubhouse with a group of campers talking to Bernie Carbo, forever enshrined in Red Sox history books for hitting that mammoth pinch-hit home run into the center field bleachers during the 1975 World Series that tied the game and set the stage for Carlton Fisk to end it. With extreme candor, Bernie told us he felt high as a kite when he came to home plate that night. "The center field fence appeared to be much closer than usual and I connected good," he told us. "It was one of the longest home runs I ever hit."

When I contacted Bernie via e-mail last year, I asked him if it was okay to write about our fantasy camp chat in my book. Bernie said that he preferred that I not write about his candor. Imagine my surprise when I arrived in my hometown of St. Johnsbury, Vermont on April 1st of 2010 and picked up a copy of the Boston Globe. On the sports page was an article and a picture of Bernie. The caption over the photo read; "I played every game high. I was addicted to anything you could possibly be addicted to. I played the outfield sometimes when it looked like the stars were falling from the sky."

Congratulations, Bernie Carbo, for being clean and sober since 1994. I remember going to a pub in Ft. Myers, just a short stroll from the Sheraton. Bernie went with us. While most of us ordered beers, he ordered water with a twist of lemon. Keep up the great work, Bernie.

Bernie was in Pembroke, New Hampshire a couple of days ago and I drove there to see him speak. His story is uplifting and it is a great example of the glory of God. Bernie Carbo turned his life over to the

Lord and now he and his wife, Tammy, are helping other people do the same thing with his Diamond Ministries. What a blessing. When he hit that home run in 1975, he was wearing a uniform with the number 1 on the back. He didn't know it then because he was still looking for love and salvation and some kind of stability in his life. He was number One in the eyes of God. It took another nineteen years and much intervention in the form of former teammates and a Baptist minister but Bernie Carbo found his way and he is today a man of conviction. God bless you, brother.

Bernie Carbo's story fits right in with the theme of this story. Love and positive thinking takes care of everything, especially addictions. I smoked for over 50 years, even after suffering from cancer and a couple of heart attacks. I finally got a strongly worded message from my higher power in May, 2006, in Santa Rosa, California, where I was undergoing treatment for my coronary artery disease. The message from god was straightforward: "Son, He said. The love of God and your wife is infinitely more powerful than your addiction to nicotine. Believe in this power and it will save your life." My good cardiologist, Dr. Greg Hopkins, advised me to take Welbutrin. On Sunday, March 18th, 2006, also Joanne's birthday, I took one tiny white pill and quit. My heart and my brain worked closely on this one, making sure I would never smoke another disgusting cigarette and I've stayed true to that conviction. And I have saved thousands of dollars in the process. Unfortunately, I was still hooked in 1994 and I shudder to think how many cigarettes I smoked at camp.

The highlight of that totally awesome week was the game that was played between the campers and the pros on Friday night at City of Palms Park, the sparkling new stadium in Ft. Myers. There were a couple of thousand people in the stands that night and each camper was introduced over the public address system by the late Ken Coleman. Each of us had an opportunity to play a position in the field and a chance to go to bat against a pro. I was a little nervous as I stepped into the batters' box. Rick Wise was on the mound. Marc Sullivan was catching. I fouled off a pitch, then I swung and missed. Marc told me to keep my eye on the ball and just let the bat meet the pitch. On the next pitch, I hit a ground ball to the left side of the pitcher's mound. As Rick Wise took a long time picking the ball up, I ran to first base and beat the throw. I was congratulated by Mike Easler. They handed me the baseball and later, Johnny Pesky signed: "Barney's first hit - Nice going, Johnny Pesky." Sixteen years later, the baseball occupies a special place in my trophy case.

Too soon, it seemed, the week was coming to an end. We all attended a going away banquet in the ballroom of the Sheraton. Awards were handed out and lots of short speeches were made by the campers and the pros. Monbouquette, Bell and Radatz got a huge round of applause as did John and Stuart Savage. Congratulations, guys. Great job.

What an awesome experience and it's one I will talk about with great pride for the rest of my life. I would love an opportunity to re-visit Red Sox Fantasy Camp someday. Perhaps that will happen after this book is published.

Eleven

Music To My Ears: A Viola

The Red Sox had acquired left hander Frank Viola in the middle of 1991. Now, in spring training, 1992, Viola was reunited with Jeff Reardon and Tom Brunansky. All three men played for the 1987 World Champion Minnesota Twins. Viola was bothered by an infected fingernail on the middle finger of his left hand which affected his curveball and a "glomus tumor" under the fingernail of his ring finger that affected his changeup. The tumor was removed after the 91 season. Now, in the Red Sox clubhouse in Winter Haven, Viola was asked about his current physical condition.

He talked rapidly with a heavy New York/New Jersey accent.

"Well, there's no question I feel good. There's no question about that. I've got movement again on my fastball. I've got movement on the change. I've got a pretty good curve and a good slider working right now. I've got four pitches now, where as soon as I grip the ball, it just feels comfortable. It was like foreign to me last year. You put all four of these together, you gotta feel good about it."

"Do you get more excited about the start of the season?" one of the writers asked.

"I'm ready for it," Viola said. "As far as exciting, the first couple of days you're excited about being down here, then you have that doldrum period. Now, you're getting to the point where you can't wait for the season to start. There's been peaks and valleys here but I've been excited the whole way through. I'd like to see us score a few more runs and get the offense going a little but other than that, it's going to be a lot of fun. I've had good Aprils in the last couple of years, going 6 and 0 then 7 and 0. I don't know if that's a National League thing or what. Up until '86 or '87, I was always a slow starter. Maybe my work ethic is different down here. Maybe I just prepare mentally a little better, but right now, the key is for me to go out each time for my 35 or 36 starts and be ready to go, just put the whole package together this year."

I asked Viola if he had to make any adjustments coming from the National League back to the American League.

"No, I'm just throwing my game again. When you have four pitches to work with and you can throw them at any time, it makes my job and everyone else's job a lot easier. The hitter's not going to be looking for one pitch at a certain time. He's going to have to be guessing the whole way through and you know that's my game. I'm not a power pitcher. I can't throw the fastball by people the way Roger can. I just have to be smart out there and mix up the pitches. As I say, when I can feel all four pitches and know I can throw them anytime, that's advantageous for me."

I was delighted to have Viola's attention. "Your pitching motion out there on the mound looks effortless from up in the press box. It doesn't look as though you're working hard."

"I've been lucky," Viola said. "I've had pretty good teaching. Everything has come pretty easy to me as far as my mechanics go. If they do go awry, it's nothing major. It's just a slight adjustment that has to be made during the course of the game. When you cut down the principle of your mechanics, the easiest way to pitch is with the least amount of effort, not going through the over-the-head windup and all that rigamarole. Everything's been able to stay together pretty good for me."

"What do you think about the pitching staff and the overall talent on this team?" another writer asked.

"Well, you gotta be excited about the way we've been throwing the ball down here. Joe's (Joe Hesketh) been throwing the ball real well. Gardy (Mike Gardiner) seems to be comfortable again. And then Roger is just Roger. He'll be ready, no matter what the situation is. That's the name of the game. If Roger and I get out of the gate quickly, it becomes repetitious. If Roger pitches well, I want to pitch better than him. It's going to be a good cycle. In middle inning relief, you've got some established veterans like Darwin, Harris, Bolton or whatever the case may be. You've got one of the best closers of all time in Reardon, so the pitching, I think, is going to be strong. It's just a question of getting out the gate quick and establishing something positive. As far as the hitters are going to go, you don't have to worry about that. You've got some quality hitters over there, Viola said, pointing to the other side of the clubhouse. They'll get some runs for us."

I asked Viola to talk about the '87 season with the Minnesota Twins. "You guys had a great team. Did you have that camaraderie, that closeness with the Twins' players that you're feeling here?"

"I think you have to, I really do. You hang out together for eight months. You'd better get along! I mean, it makes for a long-ass season." Viola's voice rose in pitch as he continued. "I'm telling you. You're laughing, but it's a serious thing. I give a lot of the credit to Tom Kelly, just being the manager he was. He gets those guys together, all 25 guys that go up north and they all know their roles. Say you're not an everyday player and you know that in the seventh or eighth inning, he's going to use you as a defensive replacement in certain situations. You might not be happy with not playing every day but at least you've got to be happy with the role he's established for you. And you know you're going to be using those roles. I like the way Butch is running this camp. I really do. He's going after you. He can be your friend. He's trying to be buddy-buddy with you. A manager, up to a certain point, can be like that. He's seeing how far we can go."

"But he can be firm," I said to Viola.

"Damn right," Viola said with emphasis. "You're going to respect the man. He's going to make sure of that and there you have it. That's how Tom Kelly started and look how successful he's been. I've had one of the best managers in Tom Kelly, in baseball and I think Butch is going to do a heck of a job with these guys."

"You have to feel good about being reunited with Reardon and Brunansky," I said to Viola.

Viola's face broke into a wide grin and he jokingly said; "That's the only bad thing. I've got Bruno and Reardon back but other than that, I'm having a great time." Viola laughed as I thanked him for the interview.

"Any time, Barney. Happy to oblige. See ya."

Jovial and outgoing. Frank Viola was just what the team would need in 1992. I left the Red Sox clubhouse feeling good about Viola's attitude. It was obvious he was delighted to be wearing a Red Sox uniform and getting an opportunity to work side by side with Roger Clemens. I had no problem visualizing 35 to 40 victories for the Clemens/Viola tandem. Oh what beautiful music.

It wasn't to be. The regular season got off to a bizarre start with a horrific lack of offense and tough losses for both Clemens and Viola in Yankee Stadium by scores of 4 to 3 and 3 to 2. Then the Red Sox traveled to Cleveland where they played and won a 19 inning marathon on Saturday, April 11th, Manager Butch Hobson used seven pitchers. On Sunday, Matt Young took the mound for the first game of a scheduled doubleheader, the only one of the year. Young, who could never master the art of holding runners on first, pitched a no-hitter for eight full innings but he also gave up 7 walks. Two of the walks were converted into runs and the Indians won the most bizarre game by a score of 2 to 1. Because of a new ruling by Commissioner Fay Vincent, the game could not be counted as a No-Hitter but the baseball went to Cooperstown anyway.

Meanwhile back in Boston, Roger Clemens was recovering from an injury to the little finger of his pitching hand. Knowing the pitching staff was depleted by the nineteen inning game, Roger phoned Butch Hobson and volunteered to fly out and pitch the second game of the doubleheader. The "Rocket Man" flew in from Boston and pitched a two-hit shutout, putting the Red Sox in the record books for allowing just two hits to the opposition in eighteen innings of baseball. Frank

Viola was absolutely correct. Roger Clemens was ready, no matter what the situation.

Hall of Famer: Jeff Reardon

Another most enjoyable interview in Winter Haven that final year was with Jeff Reardon, one of the all time great relief pitchers and a good person as well. Reardon was sitting on a stool near his locker in the corner of the Chain-O'-Lakes clubhouse. I introduced myself and told him about our positive thinking book.

"That's good," said Reardon. "This might be the year of the Red Sox."

"You were a Red Sox fan yourself," I said to Reardon, knowing he was raised in New England. "You must have been particularly happy when you came over here from the twins?"

"Yeah, that was my dream, to play for the Red Sox. So many people follow the Red Sox and they haven't won since Babe Ruth. I didn't even realize that until I signed with them but then I heard it every day."

"Well, our little book is exactly the opposite approach of Dan Shaughnessy's premise in *Curse of The Bambino*. I grew up in New England too, Jeff and maybe it's bred into us but when things are going real good, it's like 'oh my gosh,' and this cloud of collective negativity descends."

"Yeah, I think they do that a little too much, though," Reardon said. "When I grew up, they were in the playoffs a lot. They've given New England exciting teams since '67. They always say, 'Well, they're not going to win it.' It's hard to hear that all the time. That's not the reason they haven't won it. Still, you don't like to hear it as a player."

"Do you use visualization, Jeff, like the year ahead? Do you set personal goals for yourself?"

"My goal is to stay healthy, Barney. If I stay healthy, I can do what I've done for thirteen years. I visualize, hoping to get into the World Series and stuff like that. Nineteen eighty-seven was the most fun I've ever had in my life and it was miserable the first six weeks after changing leagues. The manager, Tom Kelly, stuck with me. The guys were great. I'll always remember them for that. I kept working harder and harder and from that six week period on, I had great stats, helped them to get to the World Series, then pitched in four of the five World Series games."

"It's so early, Jeff, a long road to the World Series. Do the guys talk about it?"

"You don't really talk about it," Reardon continued. "Everybody's excited because everyone thinks we've got a good chance of going all the way. You know, we picked up Viola and we already had the hitters. People say to me: 'You've been in a World Series. You've got all those saves. How do you top that? Well, the ultimate thrill would be being in the World Series with the Red Sox, whether I'm on the mound or not, just to be on that team."

"I think a lot of the fans here in Winter Haven were surprised to see you come in during the middle of the game today, Jeff."

Reardon laughed. "That was no big deal. This is spring training. I knew yesterday. I'm getting plenty of work. I've got six innings already. usually, I only pitch about eight. I'll probably wind up with fourteen or fifteen innings which is plenty."

I asked Jeff about a neck injury incurred in 1991.

"Oh, it's fine. I feel fine. I'll pitch Friday. I'll probably be a little stiff tomorrow after going two innings

today. People make a big deal out of me going two innings. I can pitch three, four, five or whatever they want me to pitch."

"Have you ever wanted to be a starter, Jeff?"

"Hey, if I wasn't a stopper, I'd like to try it. I like the role I'm in. I was a starter in the minors. I was 26 and 7, not too bad, huh."

"Not too shabby, Jeff Reardon."

Monday night, June 15th, 1992: Fenway Park

The Red Sox are leading the Yankees 1 to 0. It's the top of the ninth and Jeff Reardon is called in from the bullpen to save the game and pass Rollie Fingers for the most saves (342) meaning a trip to the Hall of Fame in Cooperstown, New York.

Reardon does the job in style before a nationwide audience on ESPN, striking out Kevin Maas, the last batter he faces. His Red Sox teammates pour out on to the field and for a brief moment, it feels as it would if they had just won the World Series. Jeff is carried over to the box seats by Roger Clemens and Frank Viola. June Reardon greets her husband with a hug and a congratulatory kiss. Once again, Red Sox fans are witnessing a moment in baseball history. The night belongs to Jeff Reardon.

Twelve

1995 was a very exciting time in my life. I felt so blessed. I had already achieved many of my boyhood dreams. I had spent a whole year at Fenway Park and attended Red Sox Fantasy Camp. I had survived a five way bypass. After losing my second wife to an incurable illness, I was lucky enough to cross paths with my soul mate who had just been out there waiting for us to meet. Joanne and I were residing in Fort Bragg where we never tired of the beautiful scenery. Some people traveled from across the world to see it. It was there for us every day, the thousands of redwood trees, the bluffs overlooking the Pacific Ocean, the inland lakes and streams, the many fine dining establishments and the people that inhabited this wonderful place.

Roberta was expecting her fourth child, another boy. She and her family, which consisted of Jeremy, Joshua and Jenna, moved to Fort Bragg from Oregon to live with us in a big old house. I mean it was big and it was old but it had character. It was a new time in America. People were buying computers. The world was changing before our eyes. There was a new buzzword called "Internet." We could push a few buttons on our computer and click on a few characters on the keyboard and read what some engineers at M.I.T. were thinking or working on. Suddenly, we could communicate with people from around the world. There were new doors opening and exciting new opportunities for thousands of people and the 21st Century was just five years away.

I had great love of radio broadcasting, an ambition that had always been with me. At Joanne's urging, I started a brand new radio program on 98.5 FM, KSAY called *The Good News Guys*, starring Fred and Barney. We had nothing to do with the Flintstones but people thought we were pretty funny and we were able to round up quite a few sponsors and have a lot of fun on the radio. We would always close our show by saying "See you on the radio," in unison. Soon, we became the talk of the town and expanded from one hour to two, five mornings a week from 7 to 9 am. My voice was recognized everywhere I went. We urged the business owners to come on the show and talk about their businesses with us and they just loved it. So did the listeners. It was radio with a twist, not just the same old thirty or sixty second commercials and then more bad news. We aired the good news and we asked people to call the show with their own good news. It just so happened that the O. J. Simpson trial was on TV and people were tired of hearing about it. Our radio program came along at just the right time.

On November 3rd, 1995, Jacob Alexander Ashman entered the world in a Fort Bragg hospital. I got to hold him when he was just twenty minutes old. I looked in his eyes and said "fuzzy chicken" and he giggled. I was thrilled. I never had any children of my own and this was the boy I had always wished for. He was beautiful.

When Jacob was a year old, we got lucky and we were able to buy property in Little River, California. We had been getting our mail in Little River for quite some time. It was a dream come true. We bought two and a half acres with two houses on the property for the quite astounding price of $150,000. It took less than thirty days for the loan to be approved. Joanne and I and the four children moved on to the property. We were thrilled, especially with the huge redwood tree right beside the cottage. What we didn't realize was that the roots of the tree had infiltrated the septic tank and that would create some plumbing problems but for the present time, everything was perfect. The owner included his tractor in the sale. It was exactly what we needed to take care of the place, start making improvements and take

Jacob for rides.

Ironically, the land where our property lay was about the area where Christine's ashes would have landed when I scattered them from a Cessna piloted by my friend and flying instructor, John Merriman. We were close to the pygmy forest and only about five minutes from the ocean and a beautiful beach. There was also a general store and post office in the same building and the beautiful Little River Inn with a nine hole golf course. Fort Bragg was a ten mile drive north.

Jacob was a year old when we bought the property. In the next six years, we taught him to hug a redwood tree and we spent many evenings telling him the moon belonged to him and we took him on a lot of tractor rides. Looking back, I would say that it was a good time for all the grandchildren. We watched in awe as Jeremy graduated from high school and Jenna grew into a beautiful young lady. Joshua was growing and searching for some direction in his life. Meanwhile, a young man named Jim Watson came riding into Ft. Bragg on a bicycle and captured Roberta's heart. The two were married on Little River Beach in 2002 and would later become proud parents of Jaci Marlo Watson, our ninth grandchild. The family is currently residing in Colorado Springs.

I was having a good time with the radio program although getting up at 5:30 in the morning didn't always agree with me. My routine was always the same. I would, shower and shave, then get into my Ford Probe and make the eleven mile drive from the house to the Chevron station where I would buy donuts, coffee, and a newspaper, the Santa Rosa Press Democrat, owned by the New York Times. I always enjoyed their sports page and I like the news items as well. Of course, I would buy a pack of Marlboro Lites if I was running low. I would smoke and drink coffee until it was time to get the radio program on the air.

I am one of the few people in the radio business that had an hour long interview with America's Sweetheart, Ms. Doris Day of Carmel, California. When Doris was still a teenager, she recorded "Sentimental Journey," accompanied by Les Brown and his Band of Renown. That was our theme song for the program. Later on, I would get acquainted with Stumpy Brown, the brother of Les and a trombone player. Stumpy lives in Palm Springs and over the years, he was a marvelous guest on my show whenever I asked him. It took several weeks, a letter and a few phone calls to make the Doris Day interview happen. In the summer of 1997, my persistence was rewarded. Joanne and I were visiting Alex Randall in the Virgin Islands when Roberta called from California to let me know that Doris had consented to the interview. The news brought tears to my eyes. The interview was one of the highlights of my career. Only the week before, John Denver had crashed his ultralight airplane into Monterey Bay, stunning the entire world. Years earlier, Doris and John had performed a television special with Denver. He is missed.

Another beautiful lady in the entertainment business became a regular guest of *The Good News Guys*. I don't recall the exact details of how Judy Collins and I got acquainted but I do remember that when I came to the radio station early one morning, the phone was ringing and it was Judy calling from New York. I was thrilled. We hit it off immediately and when I told her we were desperately in need of rain on the coast, she promised to do a rain dance with her friends. It rained a couple of weeks later. Between 1996 and 2002, Judy was on the program several times. I remember fondly the day she called us from the Brown Palace Hotel in Denver. A new book written by Judy had just come out and it included her hit, *Shameless*, also the title of the book. She sang the opening lines of the song for us without any accompaniment and it was fabulous. We were blown away. I can't say enough about this beautiful lady with a voice that has been described as "liquid silver." Over the years, she has filled with Carnegie Hall several times. She recorded a couple of songs that became synonymous with her, called *Amazing Grace, Both Sides Now*, and *Send In The Clowns*.

I was privileged to attend several of her performances as her guest. At each show, I would visit Judy backstage. When she appeared in Santa Rosa, California in 1995, I asked for and received comps for Joanne, myself and Roberta who brought Jacob with her. He was two weeks old at the time. Judy held him in her arms and we took a picture. Now, more than fourteen years later, Judy is still on tour and doing well. Bless her heart. She is a beautiful lady and I'm honored to know her.

I took a lot of pride in featuring baseball players on the program. Bobby Doerr and I knew each other quite well after meeting in 1991, then attending fantasy camp in 1994. He never turned down a request to be on the program and he always shared great stories with us. I call him often to check on him since he is now 92. Tom Brunansky was on with us many mornings from his home in the San Diego area. He was always a class act and a most entertaining guest.

There is another Baseball Hall of Famer who spends his summers on the coast where he has a home overlooking the ocean. His name is Duke Snider and he was delighted to make a personal appearance at the little radio station. I could hardly believe my good fortune. Here I was interviewing the "Duke," formerly of the beloved Brooklyn Dodgers. In North Danville, I would listen to Dodger games on a New York radio station with the inimitable Red Barber and his partner, Vin Scully, doing the broadcasts and Vin was still broadcasting Dodger games, more than sixty years later. His voice is one of the most recognizable voices in sports. "Dem Bums" is how the Dodgers were referred to in Brooklyn in their heyday. They were probably the most loved team in sports. When they moved to LA in 1958, people cried in Brooklyn. What a joy it was to have Duke on the program with me.

The radio program continued to be popular and earn good revenue as 1999 became 2000 and we entered the 21st Century without all the dire predictions coming true. Remember what they said? Our computers would be rendered totally useless and the data would be lost. There would be chaos in the world financial markets. There would be many colossal power failures. None of that happened. It was a smooth and uneventful transition.

On September 11th, 2001, the world changed as America came under attack from suicidal terrorists. I left the program a short time later because I could no longer tolerate working with the person on the other side of the radio desk. It was my choice but nothing lasts forever and it was a good time to go in another direction and change my routines. I traveled to the Virgin Islands to visit Alex Randall. We were both believers in good news radio formats. There was enough bad news. For example, the bad news from the attacks were that 5,000 people died. More than 50,000 people lived, including survivors and people who were meant to be in the buildings but were somewhere else. Alex and I attempted to get good news into mainstream radio but we were unsuccessful with our endeavors. We were trumped by something called email.

Alex Randall lives on Water Island in a beautiful home with a custom designed swimming pool and many other amenities. In the past few years, he has opened up the other cottages on his property to year round guests. When it's cold and snowy on the eastern seaboard, you can go to St. Thomas and visit Alex. No passport is required. It's a U.S. territory. It's always 80 degrees and the beaches are awesome. You can feel just like Humphrey Bogart while enjoying rum and cokes at Tickle's open-air lounge at the Crown Bay Marina. It's a good life down there in paradise. Alex and his family travel back and forth from Water Island to St. Thomas every day on their boat. Bev is a physician, specifically a baby doctor. Alex goes up the hill to WSTA while Dr. Randall takes the children to school then goes to her office.

I was looking forward to meeting Beverly Randall for the first time when I traveled to the Virgin Islands in 2001. Alex and the boys, Sander and Marshall met me at the airport, then we drove to Crown Bay Marina where we boarded the boat for the ride over to Water Island. It was getting dark as Alex was backing the boat into his docking area. I was hanging on to a metal rail on the boat when a wave pushed the boat backwards. The middle finger of my left hand was caught between two metal rails and the tip of the finger was immediately severed. I met Bev with my hand wrapped in a towel and quite a bit of bleeding happening. She applied first aid then calmly instructed Alex to take me back across the bay to the emergency room at the St. Thomas hospital where I was stitched up. It took about three hours. At one point, the attending doctor called for a "bone cutter." The only one available was in use in the operating room. As I recall, it was nearly 4 am. when we returned to the house. Now, whenever people are disembarking, Alex might say: "Don't pull a Barney."

I stayed on Water Island until just before Thanksgiving, 2001. Alex and his family were planning their annual trip to Philadelphia. It was time for me to go back to California. My finger was healing, although still pretty ugly to look at and I was anxious to get home for themselves holidays. It seemed very strange to see years that started with 20 instead of 19. The horrifying events of September had altered the world we lived in. People were apprehensive about traveling, especially flying. Anybody of middle eastern origin was a suspect. The United States had been attacked for the first time since December, 1941 and suddenly we were at war with an enemy that hated everything we stood for and they were intent on creating death and destruction, especially in heavily populated areas. There doesn't seem to be any end to this constant state of conflict between the free world and nations who want to build and use nuclear weapons. We continue to seek peace in the world, one mind at a time.

Thirteen

I turned 65 and started receiving my full social security check in 2002. My Air Force retirement and Joanne's pension from 25 years of teaching were enough to allow us to live comfortably. However, there were dark clouds on the horizon. There were root problems with the septic tank that was located between the two houses. The cottage that Joanne and I lived in was lower than the main house and during periods of heavy rain, the septic tank water would back up into our shower stall. I did a lot of bailing and a lot of cussing and I was getting sick to my stomach for no apparent reason. Roberta and Jim got married on the beach that summer and we all had a great time, dressing in Elizabethan costumes, eating turkey legs, drinking beer and generally whooping it up but I didn't look good nor did I feel good. I was very pale and drawn looking. Joanne was working as a caregiver and she would leave the house early in the morning. One morning as she was preparing to leave, I was in the bathroom, vomiting. She insisted that I get myself over to the Travis AFB hospital, a four hour drive away. I agreed and I made the drive by myself, smoking cigarettes on the way.

I checked into the emergency room and after a few tests, I was admitted. There was an unusually high amount of calcium in my system. They did further tests and they called Joanne. They didn't want to come right out and say I had cancer but they were hinting at it.

We were referred to the Oncology Department. The female physician from the Philippines delivered the grim news.

"It appears, after further testing," she said, "that you have Non-Hodgkins Lymphoma, Stage 3B. That's dangerous but the good news is that we've had very good success treating this type of cancer. The chemotherapy used has given us good results with a lot of patients."

"What are my chances?" I wanted to know.

"Fifty-fifty," she told us. "Some people sail right through this," she told us. My hand went up. "That's me," I said. I made up my mind right then and there that I was going to beat the mean, nasty invader. It was June, 2002 and the first chemo treatment would be performed as an inpatient. As I recall, it took a few hours but it was painless and uneventful. The next treatment would take place in three weeks in the Oncology lounge.

Joanne and I moved into the Fisher House on Travis AFB, across the street from the hospital. It was for people who had to take long courses of treatment for their afflictions. We qualified without any problem. We had a nice bedroom upstairs and there was no charge. Caspar was living with us. He was twelve years old and he wasn't feeling well either. Our stay at the Fisher House was very comfortable. I took a lot of naps. There was a large communal kitchen with a huge refrigerator where people kept their own juices and things. Wives from the squadrons on the base brought in baked dishes and desserts every day. We didn't have to do very much shopping.

I wrote a letter to the Ft. Bragg Advocate-News, informing them what was happening in my life. I told them about the cancer and the long-term treatment and the encouraging news about the success. Many of themselves listeners of the radio program responded with love and caring. I received some very touching mail. The entire congregation of the local Episcopal church prayed for my recovery. My chemotherapy treatments were going well. I felt stronger after each one. I lost my hair but my weight stayed steady and I had a good appetite. A very nice lady at Fisher House insisted that I eat her homemade chicken soup after every treatment. It was delicious and I think it helped. My red blood cell count stayed high. After each chemo treatment, Joanne had to give me shots in my tummy and I took steroids for seven days. The blood counts stayed perfect and I felt that I was getting better with each treatment.

Reluctantly, we put our property on the market. Our lives were being changed by the cancer and we knew that it would be difficult to maintain house payments. The property needed about $25,000 worth of improvements and we were in no position to afford the costs. Originally, our next door neighbor, Bill, was interested, but he had to back out. However, he had friends that were interested. We listed the property for $300,000, twice what we paid in 1996. The prospective buyers accepted the offer. We didn't need to hire a realtor, so we had no commissions to pay. It was a good deal.

One afternoon, as I was seated in a big comfortable chair in Oncology, being given a chemo treatment, the nurse handed me the phone and said "I think your wife just bought a motor home." It was true. Joanne had found a clean, one-owner 1990 Tioga with only a few thousand miles on it. The owner wanted $17,500. Joanne offered him $15,000 cash and he took the offer.

In September, we went home to get the property ready to sell. I could only lay around and watch everyone else work. While I was just laying around, I got a high fever. Joanne took me to the hospital. I was feeling very sick. I had pneumonia. They must have given me every drug that was available because in seven days, I felt rejuvenated. The pneumonia was gone.

We had to take our cats to the local humane society which made me very sad. It seemed very unfair but there wasn't much I could do about it. Our beloved Caspar stayed with us. When we took him to a vet to be examined, we learned he had Non-Hodgkins Lymphoma, the same cancer that I had. Ultimately, we had to have him put to sleep. He was so good. I remember how he clung to me the night before as if to let me know that he understood everything about life and about leaving it behind for a better place where there would be no pain and suffering. It was like losing a family member. He would stay in our hearts forever.

The transaction for the sale of our beautiful property went through and by the time we paid bills, we had about $42,000 in the bank. We flew to Boston, then drove up to Vermont. I wanted to see my high school classmates, perhaps for the last time. I loved being back in Danville, if only for a few days. Arnie and Winona Gadapee were so gracious, as they always are. It was great to see many others as well, including Rodney Daniels and Neil Randall. Rodney is President Emeritus of the Passumpsic Savings and Loan Bank and he has done well for himself, despite rooting for the St. Louis Cardinals. I loved growing up with the Daniels family next door.

The Lord works in amazing ways. I am so blessed to be here in my home state again, eight years later. This time, the cancer is far behind me. I'm a survivor in more ways than one.

I survived because I used my heart and my mind to defeat the illness. I never claimed it. I used the awesome power of visualization and communication. I spoke to the trillions of cells within my body, telling them the sheriff's posse was coming to get them and if the bad cancer cells knew what was good for them, they had better get out of my body. Isn't that pretty amazing? Each of the microscopic cells in our bodies have substance! Deepak Chopra says the cells are distinct universes in themselves. He also says thoughts are very powerful. The scientific world now agrees that thoughts have energy. If you're sick and you believe with all your heart that you can make yourself better, then just go ahead and do it!

When I finally quit smoking in 2006, after the cancer and after two heart attacks in 2005 and 2006, I used the same techniques. I visualized myself without a cigarette in my hand. I took one tiny pill called Welbutrin and I instructed the endorphins in my brain to shut down their craving for nicotine. They thought they were getting a high from the nicotine. They weren't. The smoke and the nicotine were killing me. It was a slow form of strangulation. I am now totally unhooked from the disgusting, smelly habit and the relationship with my wife is so much better. And I have saved a few dollars by not buying cigarettes which are now nearly $7 a pack for some brands.

By December, 2002, I felt so good that we were able to travel to Hawaii with the Air Force. We spent a couple of weeks in comfortable lodgings at Hickam AFB, Hawaii. The warm trade winds were wonderful. I did a lot of walking, especially from our room to the commissary for groceries.

In January, 2003, we received the good news. After undergoing a full body scan in Sacramento, I was told there was no evidence of any tumors. I was in 100% remission.

We assumed our vagabond life in 2003. We let Jim and Roberta use our motor home until they could find a permanent place to live. Joanne's ex son-in-law was in China, recovering from Hepatitis and making a whole new life for himself after separating from Lori, Joanne's oldest daughter. He invited Joanne to come to China to teach English and help pay the rent on his two bedroom apartment.

I followed the Red Sox faithfully, right up to the night that Aaron Boone hit a home run that ended the season for the Red Sox. It was nearly as disgusting as Dent's pop fly in 1978. Shortly after the season ended, I flew to Hong Kong to be with Joanne. After landing, we made our way to the Chunking Mansion, a really cheap ten story hotel in the heart of Hong Kong. It has a lot of tiny rooms and an eclectic mix of guests, primarily from India and Africa. The elevators were always an adventure. There were only two elevators and they were very small. Sometimes, there would be a lot of people lined up with their suitcases, waiting to get on the elevator. When it was full, it was scary as it creaked and groaned upward.

Our room was very small, a bed with a little space beside it and a shower that was very tiny. When we turned on the shower, the toilet got a shower as well. You can see the Chunking mansion on the Internet. Just go to *Chunking-Mansion.hk*.

There was a big celebration scheduled in Hong Kong the second night we were there. There were thousands of people in the streets. I was wearing Bermuda shorts with deep side pockets and I made the mistake of not buttoning my pocket. When we returned to our room after watching fireworks over Hong Kong harbor, I discovered, to my dismay, that my wallet was gone. It was a sickening feeling. My military ID card, a couple of credit cards and my driver's license were all gone. Luckily, there was very little cash in the wallet. Incredibly, months later, after we were living in China, we got word in the United States that the wallet had been recovered by Hong Kong police where we had filed a report. Roberta was our emergency contact and she received word that the wallet and all the documents were found. Absolutely amazing. My good friend, Tim, made a special trip to Hong Kong to get it back and he bought me a new wallet which I am still using today.

At the Mansion, we discovered two young men from Ghana who were working at the hotel, making up rooms and handling guest services. We took an immediate liking to them. We found out they weren't making much money and they were forced to sleep on the floor or a sofa at night. Samee and Boni wanted to get to China so they could get teaching jobs. We decided to help them do that.

Boni's wife, Irene, was expecting their first child in Ghana. Boni didn't know when the baby would be born but Joanne knew. She told him it would be a girl and she will be born very soon. Amazingly, Joanne was right. The baby was born a couple of days later. It was a girl and they named her Joanne. We became the Godparents. We paid the hundred dollar fee and got our visas for entry into China, then along with the two young men, we boarded a train for Shenzhen, China. The first thing one discovers about China is that there are a lot of people. The second thing one discovers is that somebody is always trying to sell you something, especially the taxi drivers. As soon as they discover you don't speak Chinese, the price goes up. We learned it was always advisable to have a Chinese friend with us to negotiate the fares or have the cell phone number of a Chinese friend, call him and just hand the phone to the driver.

Boni and Samee both got jobs. Today, Samee is married to a Chinese girl and they have a young son. He is doing well in the furniture export business. Boni is in Japan and he has never returned to Ghana. He has never seen his daughter who will be 7 years old this October.

We became close friends with Tim and Wendy, a delightful young Chinese couple who are boyfriend and girlfriend. They have never married. We moved into a two bedroom apartment in a 17th floor high rise with them. Wendy is so cute. She is diminutive and when she gets excited, she jumps up and down. She had befriended Joanne before I arrived in China. Once, Wendy took Joanne on a twelve hour bus ride deep into the countryside to visit Wendy's parents and her grandmother. Joanne was the first white person to visit the remote village. She was treated with great respect. Wendy's family catered to her every need, always making sure she was comfortable.

Tim and Wendy were awesome young people. Tim was a terrific chef. We always enjoyed dinner in the apartment. We felt relaxed and comfortable around them and they were our interpreters whenever we needed those services. When we left China in January of 2004, we told them we would return. We planned to go to China in October or November this year, 2010.

2004 was upon us and what a year it promised to be. Our good friend, Jim Wagoner, owned a manufactured home on an acre of land in Moffat, Colorado, a tiny settlement in the middle of the Sangre De Cristo valley. Actually, Jim's place was between Moffat and Villa Grove. I will never forget how spectacular the star viewing was in that special place. The altitude was 7,000 feet, so I definitely felt closer to the starry heavens.

Joanne had chosen to return to California after we had a little disagreement. She left me with the motor home. Most of the time, I was afraid to go anywhere because the tires were so worn. It was nearly 30 miles from Jim's place to Salida, the nearest town of any size. I prayed wouldn't have a blowout every time I made the trip. I was lucky. I only had to buy one tire all summer. There was another problem with the vehicle. The engine would get hot and there would be a "vapor lock." and it would just stop running. I usually had to wait at least thirty minutes for it to cool down. It wasn't fun. There is nothing worse or more frustrating than vehicle problems in the middle of nowhere.

Of course, I was following the Red Sox and they were playing pretty well. In June, I decided to go to Danville for my 50th class reunion. Out of 21 graduating seniors, eighteen of us were alive and doing well. I had attended every reunion, every five years since 1989. We had our get-together in a camp that belongs to Fran and Gracia Berwick at Joe's pond in West Danville. The weather was perfect. There were ten of us there, including Mabel Rollins, who was, in my opinion, the prettiest cheerleader in our school. In 2004, she was a sweet little lady with silver white hair. I'm sorry to report that Mabel has since passed away. Last year, we had our 55th reunion at the church in Danville. My good friend, Arnie Gadapee and I are already looking forward to our 60th in 2014. We must be doing something right.

The Red Sox were scuffling along, seven and a half games behind the Yankees by June 30th, and I wasn't feeling good about the rest of the season. I was at Jan Hatch's comfortable home in Athol, Massachusetts. Jan is my brother-in-law and over the years, he and I have had a lot of fun analyzing the strengths and weaknesses of the ball club. We've also exchanged dozens of phone calls, most of them prompted by a spectacular Red Sox game. They would win in thrilling fashion and I would call him. He would usually answer by laughing and saying, "I knew it was you when the phone rang." I used to kid him about keeping his arm in shape because the team might need him but now that he's in his sixties and I'm in my seventies, we are both past our prime. We are content to discuss the ups and downs of the team. In that magical season of 2004, there were a lot of ups and downs.

The biggest news of the season happened toward the end of July at the trading deadline when the young general manager, Theo Epstein, traded Nomar Garciaparra in a move that rocked the foundations of Red Sox Nation. Orlando Cabrera and Doug Mientkiewicz came to Boston, also Dave Roberts, a speedster from the Dodgers. The immediate reaction from the media was mostly negative and it stayed that way until the team got red, searing hot in August. All of a sudden, they were 24 games over .500 and only three games behind the hated Yankees. There was much reason for optimism. I returned to the little house on the prairie in Moffat and resumed my daily activities of driving the motor home to Villa Grove to get coffee, cigarettes and a newspaper. Then, I would hang out with Jim's dogs until early evening. The Democrats were having their convention in Chicago and I told Jim that the man who delivered the keynote address, Barrack Obama, was going to become the President someday. When he was elected in 2008, Jim remembered that I had told him that and he thought it was pretty special.

If the Red Sox were going to be on ESPN, that gave me an excuse to drive to Salida to a damned good sports bar. Quite often, I would be the only Red Sox addict in the place and while the TV sets over the bar were tuned to the Colorado Rockies, I would have a big screen TV in the corner of the room tuned to a Red Sox game. I would devour a big juicy hamburger, a plate of fries and a couple of beers. If the Red Sox won, I would return to Moffat, a very happy man.

The clear, cool nights in the valley were astounding. The Milky Way dominated the late night skies in a way I had never observed. For the first time in my life, I felt I was part of a fascinating universe that was constantly showing me planets and galaxies and extraordinary celestial events. As I gazed upwards, I would think of Ted Williams and ask him to bring the Red Sox a World Championship. I knew he was aware of the earthly happenings and somehow, I felt he could exert some heavenly influence on the outcome of the pennant race.

Meanwhile, I continued to smoke Marlboros with no thought of what damage I might be doing to my fragile arteries. I was seeing a doctor in Salida and she suggested I undergo a colonoscopy, something I had been avoiding for years.

The colonoscopy would not happen. I watched, in total amazement, as the Red Sox beat the Anaheim Angels and earned the right to play the Yankees in the American League Championship Series. Again, I watched, in utter amazement, as the Red Sox came back from a 3 games to none deficit to win the next 4 games against the Yankees and move on to the 2004 World Series!

The Yankees had pummeled the Red Sox by a score of 19 to 8. That happened on a Saturday night. The Yankees were up three games to none and they were cruising. I called Joanne and told her the season was over and that the Yankees would end it on Sunday. She told me not to give up hope. I was listening to the fourth game on the radio in the motor home. I couldn't bear to watch on television. When David Ortiz homered and won the game, I let out a whoop. I listened to the game again the next night when Ortiz singled in the bottom of the 14th inning and won the game. I watched the sixth game on the giant screen at the Ft. Carson club. Curt Schilling held the Yankees to just six hits and Mark Bellhorn homered as the Red Sox evened the Series at three games apiece. Absolutely mind boggling baseball! Prior to Game 7, I told myself that if the Red Sox won, I was going back east to Athol to watch the World Series at Jan's house. It was no contest. Johnny Damon and Derek Lowe were heroes. I watched the game on the giant screen and loved every minute of it. The Yankees and their fans were stunned. Their season was over and for the third time in my lifetime, the Red Sox were preparing to play the St. Louis Cardinals in the World Series. I called the doctor and canceled the appointment for the colonoscopy, then caught a hop with the Air Force from Peterson AFB, Colorado to Andrews AFB, Maryland. Jan met me when I got off the train in Worcester. We went to a nearby Applebee's for dinner and some libations. I had never seen such an outpouring of happiness and excitement in New England. People were just deliriously happy and it was fun to see.

We all know the result. What a kick. On Halloween night, 2004, the Red Sox put away the St. Louis cardinals to wrap up a World Championship. Joanne and I knew it was coming. We just weren't sure what year.

This is almost the end of this story. In 2005, I suffered my first heart attack in Colorado. I was hospitalized for three weeks and a lot of people, including doctors thought I wouldn't survive but I fooled them all. In 2007, while living in Nevada, I suffered my third heart attack and had to be airlifted to a Las Vegas hospital. At the time, I had a pacemaker that had been implanted in Colorado Springs. Doctors in Las Vegas decided to outfit me with a combination pacemaker and defibrillator. I had no prior knowledge of their decision. Obviously, they were required to put me under for the fairly straightforward routine procedure. There's no such thing as "routine" when you are anesthetized. You are at risk!

I woke up with a breathing device in my mouth, unable to speak until it was removed. "What happened to me?" I wanted to know.

One of the attending physicians explained. "While we were doing the procedure, you conked out. Your blood pressure went to zero and all electrical activity ceased for just over two minutes. We declared a "code blue" and were getting ready to use paddles when you recovered."

"Thank you for bringing me back," I said.

"No," the doctor said. "You brought yourself back."

Wow, I thought to myself. I died for two whole minutes, then elected to re-join the living. I had a lot more living to do, including moving back to Colorado and then coming back to Vermont to finish the book. Thank you, God. I understand.

Fourteen

I love writing. I love being creative and finding a way to express a thought in easily understandable words so that a potential reader will enjoy what they're reading. I have a good feeling about this story. I think people will read it and hopefully, they will read it to their children, the future Red Sox fans.

A few nights ago, Joanne and I went out to dinner at the River Garden restaurant here in East Burke. We were celebrating completion of the book. We had a table for two in the back room of the restaurant and in the same room, there was a large table where seven or eight people arrived for dinner. We couldn't help but overhear the conversation and it was all about the Red Sox. When I heard the names of a couple of former players who were at fantasy camp with me in 1994, I went over to the table and introduced myself. Now, I have a business card from an East Burke gentleman who works as a C.P.A. In St. Johnsbury. I will be contacting him.

It seems that the more I write, the more there is to write.

Back in 2004, I was at Jan's house and the first game of the World Series would be starting in a few hours. I decided to call Johnny Pesky. I knew a lot of people wanted to talk to him, including WEEI, the New York Times, the Boston Globe, the Boston Herald, in addition to ESPN, Johnny's many friends and former teammates. I dialed his number and got through on the fourth attempt.

"Johnny, this is Barney," I said. "Congratulations on going to the World Series. I know you're excited."

"Yeah, I'm getting ready to go to the ballpark, but my phone keeps ringing. Where are you, Barn?"

I told Johnny I was in Athol and my thoughts would be with him. "I've finally got an ending for my book," I told Johnny. He laughed and thanked me for the call. I thanked him for taking time to answer. I feel so honored to know Johnny. The book would be dedicated to him, just as Joanne and I planned it in 1991.

Of course, the Red Sox won the World Series and they handed the trophy to Johnny in the delirious clubhouse after the victory. Johnny held the trophy aloft and said; "This one's for you, Ted."

I submit that Ted Williams could very well have had a hand in guiding the Red Sox to victory. Even though he left us in 2003, his spirit remains with us. It's evident everywhere, from the statue at Fenway, at Logan Airport, at the tunnel that bears his name, at the Hitter's Hall of Fame in Florida, at the Hall of Fame in Cooperstown, at the New England Sports Museum and in San Diego, especially at Hoover High School where it all began. Ted Williams cast a large shadow. Collective belief in angels has never been higher than it is today and there is positive evidence that there's something powerful in much of the phenomena that occurs on a daily basis.

Everyone has their own belief platform, so there's a choice. Believe in the afterlife and the endless possibilities and have fun with it. How many of you have had events in your life where relatives show up at the darnedest times and places trying to tell you about the other side? The Creator answers prayers. How many people do you think were praying for a miracle in Massachusetts after the Red Sox had lost the first three games of the series to the Yankees? Almost everyone had thrown in the towel that night after the Saturday Night Massacre.

My buddy, Scott Coen, of Fox TV in Springfield, Massachusetts was with all the other media people covering the Red Sox. Many people had already left the park, fearing the season was over, so the guys and gals in the press corps moved downstairs, occupying field level box seats. Scott said they talked about how much fun the season had been, assuming that the Yankees were wrapping it up, until, until, until.........Dave Roberts stole second base. In that instant, everything changed. That's part of the beauty of the game of baseball. Things can change in a split second.

The Red Sox were named "Sportsmen of The Year" for 2004 by Sports Illustrated in the December 6th issue. Inside, there are numerous stories touching lives with touching stories to tell about generations of families rooted to the Red Sox, year after year after year, even passing through decades. If you were born in New England, chances are your whole family roots for the Red Sox.

In that historic issue, there was a heart-rendering story of Mr. George Sumner, a resident of Waltham, Mass., and a lifelong Red Sox fan:

> On October 25, the Sox were two victories away from winning the World Series when doctors sent George Sumner home to die. There was nothing more they could do for him. At home though, George Sumner's stomach began filling up with fluid and he was rushed back to the hospital. The doctors did what they could. They said he was in such bad shape that they were uncertain if he could survive the ride back home.
>
> Suddenly, his eyes still closed, George pointed to a corner of the room as if someone was there, and said, "Nope, not yet."
>
> And then George went back home to Waltham. Daughter Leah Storey knew that every day and every game were precious. She prayed hard for asleep.
>
> On the morning of Game 4, which stood to be the highlight of Jaime Andrew's life as a "pathetic," obsessed Red Sox fan, his wife, Alice, went into labor. Here it was: the conflict Jaime had feared all summer. At 2:30 PM, he took her into South Shore Hospital where they were greeted by nurses wearing Red Sox jerseys over their scrubs.

At 8:25 PM, Alice was in the delivery room. There was a TV in the room. The game in St. Louis was about to begin.

"Turn on the game."

It was Alice who wanted the TV on. Damon, the leadoff hitter, stepped into the batter's box.

"Johnny Damon!" Alice exclaimed. "He'll hit a home run."

And Damon, his long brown locks flowing out the back of his batting helmet, did just that.

The Red Sox led 3 – 0 in the bottom of the fifth inning when the Cardinals put a runner on third base with one out. Jaime could not stand the anxiety. His head hurt. He was having difficulty breathing. He broke out in hives. It was too much to take. He asked Alice to turn off the television. Alice insisted they watch until the end of the inning. They saw Lowe pitch out of the jam. Jaime nervously clicked off the TV.

At home in Waltham, George Sumner slipped in and out of sleep. His eyes were alert when the game was on, but when an inning ended, he would say in a whisper, which was all he could muster, "Wake me up when the game comes back on." Each time, no one could be certain if he would ever open his eyes again.

The Red Sox held their 3-0 lead and the TV remained off in the delivery room of the South Shore Hospital. At 11:27 PM, Alice gave birth to a beautiful boy. Jaime noticed that the baby had unusually long hair down the back of his neck. The nurses cleaned and measured the boy. Jamie was still nervous.

"Can I check the TV for the final score?" he asked Alice.

"Sure." she said.

It was 11:40 PM. The Red Sox were jumping upon

one another in the middle of the diamond. They were world champions.

George Sumner had waited a lifetime to see this – 79 years, to be exact, the last three while fighting cancer. He drew upon whatever strength was left in his body and in the loudest whisper that was possible, he said, "Yippee."

And then he closed his eyes and went to sleep.

"It was probably the last real conscious moment he had," Leah says.

George opened his eyes one last time the next day. When he saw that he was surrounded by his extended family, he said, "Hi," then went back to sleep for the final time.

George Sumner, avid Red Sox fan, passed away at 2:30 PM on October 29th. He was laid to rest with full military honors on November 2nd.

On the day that George Sumner died, Alice and Jaime Andrews took home a healthy baby boy. They named him Damon.

The Bullpen

In the June 1st, 2010 edition of my hometown newspaper, the *Caledonian Record* of St. Johnsbury, Vermont is an article about me, accompanied by a head and shoulders photograph of me "working," and wearing the top part of my Red Sox uniform. The article was written by Amy Ash Nixon and she surprised me by putting it on the front page. Nicely done, Amy.

>NEK Native, Red Sox Fan Comes Home To Write Book

East Burke – Elmer J. Barney Jr. - he goes by "E.J." - has come home to northern Vermont this summer with his wife, Joanne, something he's been wanting to do for years.

Barney is a man on a mission.

He is hoping the healthy, fresh air and inspiration of his boyhood home will help him finish up a book he's been at work on for a long time.

It is a story about baseball, specifically about the Boston Red Sox, whom E.J. adores – and has since his childhood when the family moved from North Danville during World War II to a housing project in

East Boston and his dad, Elmer Sr., took him to Fenway Park.

It is also a story about survival. E.J. Has survived a five-way bypass, multiple heart attacks and cancer.

He will share stories from his book, which he's hoping to soon publish, at the Elks Lodge in St. Johnsbury on June 10 at 6:30 p.m. The event will help kick off a fundraiser for the Caledonia County Relay For Life held at St. Johnsbury Academy's track that weekend.

Admission to E.J.'s event will be by donation, and all proceeds will benefit the American cancer Society. A raffle will be conducted to win a pair of Red Sox tickets.

"It's amazing that we have a cancer survivor, Elmer Barney, to help us kick off the Relay Weekend with this event at the Elks," relay organizer Fred Laferriere said Friday.

"Mr. Barney is a true inspiration," said Tina Keach, Elks Lodge manager. "The Elks are honored to host this special event to begin the relay weekend."

E.J. Barney – yes, he is related to the well-known late judge, Albert W. Barney. They were cousins. He feels like one lucky man, and that, he said, is more than mere happenstance.

He said a friend who lives in the Virgin Islands who is a radio broadcaster, as E.J. once was, "did an astrological thing on his computer for my birth date and it came up as a perfect double shrine." [That should be *double trine*.] It looks like the Star of David. Each one was 60 degrees apart. He told me, "You're the luckiest man on Earth."

E.J., during an interview at the Burke Mountain condo he and Joanne are renting for the summer said, "I probably am."

After his bypass, cancer, four heart attacks, having both carotid arteries operated on, Type II diabetes, pneumonia and more...yes, he is a lucky man indeed.

A retired Air Force man who spent 20 years in the military following his graduation from Danville High School, E.J. Did go on to realize his high school dream – noted in his yearbook – to become a broadcaster. He and a good friend launched a radio show in California, where he lived, called *The Good News Guys*.

Later, when E.J. Was diagnosed with Non-Hodgkins Lymphoma, his listeners would call in to tell him they were praying for him. It meant a lot.

"Seven years ago when I had cancer, I came to Vermont and had a gathering with my friends in Danville because I thought it was my last go -round," he said. "I didn't know whether I'd survive or not."

Joanne, his wife since 1988, loading the dishwasher, turned and smiled knowingly. "I knew, they tell you all about positive thinking and visualizations," she said.

E.J. said he had a way of communicating with the cells in his body, warning them the sheriff and his posse were on their way, and they'd better clear out.

E.J. Said when he went through the six months of chemotherapy at Travis Air Force Base in California, doctors told him he had the "right kind of cancer" because it was very treatable and very curable, and he had a 50/50 chance.

"The doctor said, 'Some people sail right through this,' and I raised my hand and said, 'That's me!' and I sailed right through it for six months and all the tumors went away."

At 73, and home this time not to say goodbye to his boyhood chums, but rather to say hello, E.J. Is ready to roll up his sleeves and finish his autobiography at long last, and his childhood memories are buoying his spirits.

"I was just a little kid, and starting when I was 8 years old, I idolized Ted Williams," E.J. Said of his boyhood visits to Fenway Park.

When he would go to Fenway Park, he would look up at the press box and hear the typewriters going and see the cigar smoke coming out. "I wanted to be up there," he said.

The family returned to North Danville after the war, and in 1954, after graduating from Danville High School, he caught a bus in front of Parker Drug Store and went to Manchester, N.H., and into the Air Force.

"I stayed for twenty years," he said.

His life and work have taken him overseas, to Saudi Arabia, to China, to California and Colorado and now home to Vermont.

Through it all, E.J.'s obsession with the Red Sox remained.

"It was a couple of years after we got married, and when I was writing about the Red Sox, and Joanne said, 'If you want to write about the Red Sox, you should go where they are.' That's what we did. We sold everything and took our cat and made our way to Winter Haven, Florida with a camera and notepad, and I went to Red Sox spring training with my little Sony tape recorder."

The book is called *Love Those Red Sox: One Man's Baseball Journey*.

The couple followed the team to Boston in 1991, and that was the year E.J. thought they'd win the World Series, though that wouldn't come for another 13 years.

"I thought this was the year they are going to win,"

E.J. Said. "It was the 50th anniversary of ted Williams hitting .406. It didn't quite work out that way."

When E.J. showed up to cover the Red Sox, he thought the fact he planned to write a book would be enough, but it wasn't. He was sent away. A friend (Johnny Pesky) said he must know someone in California who could help him. There had been a little publishing company near the radio station where he'd worked, and he called them. They backed him up and sent a fax to the team, and he got his credentials.

"So they let me into the ball park," said E.J., smiling ear to ear like it was yesterday. "The first time, on opening day, I was 54 years old and that just made all those dreams I had when I was 11 thinking what it would be like to be in that press box come true. The following year, 1992, it was like God said, 'OK, now you've had your fun, now I'm going to give you a real challenge.'"

E.J. Felt numbness in his wrist and they rushed to Travis Air Force Base in Fairfield, California, where he found out he needed a five-way bypass.

A decade later came the cancer diagnosis.

The book has had to take a back seat many times due to his serious, recurring health problems.

Most recently, the couple had been living in Colorado, but the high altitude made it hard for E.J. to breathe, and he and Joanne decided this was the summer to come home to Vermont.

"All these years, I've been wanting to come back to Vermont [and] I would say to Joanne, 'Oh I want to spend a summer in Vermont, I want to go home, I want to go to Willoughby Lake and have a picnic,' so finally this year, 2010, we are here. I feel totally rejuvenated," he said.

> Of being home, and being ready to finally wrap up his book, E.J. Said, "I'm in the place where I need to be. The Red Sox are all over the place!"

Thank you so much, Amy Nixon. I knew there was a reason why we met at Dunkin Donuts in St. Johnsbury. You're a terrific writer and equally terrific reporter.

Our grandson, Jacob, came to Vermont to visit us this summer. He flew from Denver to Boston on Jet Blue. It was his first flight and he loved it. He wore me out the next day as we toured Boston, including the Science Museum and the top of the Prudential Center. The next day, we brought him up here to Vermont where he stayed for nearly three weeks. Again, he wore me out. We toured Ben & Jerry's and went to the Trapp Family Lodge in Stowe on the same day. Later, I took him over to nearby Cannon Mountain and the Aerial Tramway, then we went to The Flume. I walked more than I had walked in ten years. I will be ready to go again when he returns next summer.

The evening at the Elks went well even though sparsely attended. Joanne and Jacob were there, also Arnie and Winona Gadapee. I wore my Red Sox uniform and talked about the story. Jacob and I attended the Relay For Life to benefit the American cancer Society and yes, he wore me out again. It must be really great to be fourteen and be so endowed with energy.

Joanne says to be sure and tell the readers we root for two teams, the Red Sox and whatever team is beating the Yankees.

Oh yes, there was one bit of medical information I failed to mention in the narrative. In 1996, I had both carotid arteries operated on. They were pretty plugged up and the surgery probably prevented a stroke. I have certainly dodged a few bullets in this lifetime and who knows, I may get to dodge a few more before I depart for the great baseball stadium in the sky.

East Burke, Vermont. July 25th, 2010.

August 20, 2010: Sorrow

I am still in a state of shock and grief after the passing of my dear wife, Joanne, just eighteen days ago. I have tried to fill the emptiness in my heart by doing fun things like going to a Red Sox game at Fenway Park.

Even though I am working on getting press credentials, I decided to purchase a ticket for the game between the Angels and the Red Sox on Thursday, June 19th. Alas, the home team went down to defeat but what a great time I had.

I enjoyed a few drinks before game time at a nearby sports bar that filled up as it got closer to 5pm when the gates would open. I wanted to be inside to watch some of the pre-game festivities. The first thing I saw that boggled my mind was how many people were on the field, other than players. There must have been a hundred men and women behind the rope barrier that prevents people from getting close to the batting cage.

I'm certain that is for safety reasons. Back in 1991, things were a lot different. There were only a few people on the field and it was pretty easy to get close to the batting cage and the players. Now, the players are shielded and protected. If I want to interview a player, I have to go through the Red Sox media relations department and get approval for the interview.

As I was making my way toward my seat in Section 14, I saw Peter Gammons coming toward me. I spoke to him briefly because he was in a hurry. I told him we had met in Winter Haven in 1991, and that I had finished my book project. I also told him that it was awesome to see him come back from the brain tumor that had felled him a few years ago. Peter is a regular host on NESN with Tom Caron. He is in the Hall of fame in Cooperstown after an illustrious career with the Boston Globe and ESPN. He is a damned good sportswriter and reporter. Peter's comment: "Here I am."

The beauty of Fenway Park is timeless. The ballpark was built in 1912, then re-constructed in 1934. It is breathtakingly beautiful. The green dominates. The brilliant green grass of the outfield. The infamous 37-foot-high "Green Monster," now with seats on the top, instead of the nets. The addition of upper pavilion seats atop the left field and right field grandstands have increased the seating capacity. The only down side to the evening was the fact that the Angels won the game and the old wooden seats felt really hard by the fifth or sixth inning. Next time, I will bring a seat cushion with me. I was in seat number 7 in Row NN in Box 107 on the first base line. The gentleman in the seat beside me was very large and probably would have been more comfortable with a double-wide seat. The man on my right introduced himself as Tim and I said "I'm
Barney." He and his buddy were both beer drinkers and Tim was kind enough to share his peanuts with me.

Josh Beckett was cruising along with a two-hitter until the sixth inning when L.A. tied the score, 1 to 1. Hideki Matsui came to the plate with two men on base. I told Tim that I didn't like the vibes I was getting from Matsui. On Beckett's next pitch, Matsui deposited the baseball into the right field bleacher seats. Tim said to his buddy: "Barney called the shot." Funny moment at Fenway. I left shortly afterwards since my whole body was feeling numb from the hard wooden seat. I still enjoyed the outing very much.

The Toronto Bluejays came to town today, Friday, August 20th and beat up on Jon Lester and several other pitchers. In the end, it was 16 to 2 and hundreds of TV sets were turned off across New England long before the game was over.

So, this entire weird season of 2010 has come down to a three game series with the Tampa Bay Rays. They became a much better team after they dropped the "Devil" from their name. Somehow, that just seems to be exactly right. The Rays have pitching and defense, but their offense is vulnerable. A great pitcher like Jon Lester or Clay Buchholz can beat these guys. The Red Sox must win the upcoming three game series in order to have any chance to make the playoffs.

To say that the 2010 season has been "weird" is an understatement. The injuries have been constant, from April to August. Jacoby Ellsbury, the fleet centerfielder who the Red Sox were counting on to be a leadoff hitter would terrorize opposing pitchers with his speed once he reached first base. All that wishful thinking went up in smoke when Jacoby collided with Adrian Beltre while pursuing a foul ball. Several of his ribs were cracked. Now, it's the critical time of the year and Jacoby is still not right. Jason Varitek was enjoying a resurgence at the plate until he suffered a broken toe. Victor Martinez suffered the same fate. Then, just when we thought the injury situation could not get any worse, it did. Dustin Pedroia, the sparkplug second baseman and a team leader fouled a ball off his foot and broke the "navicular" bone. Down went Dustin. He made a brief comeback and discovered that the foot was not healed. Now, he has had season-ending surgery and the prospects of the Red Sox making the playoffs are dim, very dim.

August 27-28, 2010

Tonight, Victor Martinez was a hero in St. Petersburg, powering the Red Sox to a crucial 3 to 1 victory over Tampa Bay. He did it by hitting two home runs. Hope springs eternal across New England. Despite all the injuries and despite the weirdness of this season, this team has found a way to get into the pennant race. It's the 27th of August and all is well in the heart of Red Sox country. Tomorrow, young Clay Buchholz pitches for the Sox against Matt Garza who is always tough on Boston. The good news tonight is that the Yankees are getting pounded by the Chicago White Sox. When all the dust settles, the Red Sox could be four and a half games behind the Rays and the Yankees.

It's a Sunday night in New England and the Red Sox quest for the playoffs is probably finished. They lost to the Rays tonight by a score of 5 to 3, finishing the season for all practical purposes.

September, 2010

Fast forward to September. Like the horses approaching the finish line, several teams are in the running to get to the playoffs and as usual, the American League East probably has the best teams. The Red Sox have sprung back to life by virtue of winning the last two games against the Orioles. There are six home games coming up this first weekend in September. Manny Ramirez returns to Fenway Park in a White Sox uniform. That will be entertaining to say the least. I'm sure there will be a mixture of cheers and boos to welcome him back.

I have pretty much abandoned my quest to get credentials for Fenway Park. I have to travel to Colorado and California this month and will probably leave Vermont in mid-September. Yesterday, I picked up my new business cards from Silver Mountain Graphics in St. Johnsbury and I like them. The book title is in red letters, then "A Story about Baseball & Life by E.J. & Joanne Barney" is in white lettering below that. My cell phone number and email address are at the bottom of the card which has four baseballs flying out of Fenway Park in the background. I wanted to make sure that Joanne received credit for writing this book and she will.

While in the Boston area, I stayed at Hanscom AFB Inn. I would have my breakfast at the base bowling alley where there was a framed piece on the wall near the exit that was called "Speaking of Baseball." I was struck by the fact that baseball always seems to be near me or some reference to it no matter where I go. Here are the thoughts of a few people in the game:

"It's just throwing and catching and hitting and running. What's simpler than that?"
    Paul Richards, (Orioles Manager: 1955-61) Mr. Richards also managed the Go-Go White Sox where Sam Mele played with Minoso and Rivera.

"Kids are always chasing rainbows but baseball is a world where you can catch them."
    Johnny Vander Meer (Cincinnati Reds: 1937-49)

"Baseball players are the weirdest of all. I think it's all that organ music."
    Peter Gent (author)

"As a nation, we are dedicated to being physically fit - And parking as close to the stadium as possible."
    Bill Vaughn (K.C. Star - 1981)

"Most slumps are like the common cold. They last two weeks no matter what you do."
    Terry Kennedy/ San Diego Padres catcher (1981-86)

"Thou shalt not steal. I mean defensively. On offense, indeed thou shall steal and thou must."
    Branch Rickey (Dodgers General Manager, 1943-50)

"All pitchers are liars or crybabies."
    Yogi Berra/ Yankees: 1947-63)

"It helps if the hitter thinks you're a little crazy."
    Nolan Ryan/ Houston Astros: (1980-88)

"If you don't play to win, why keep score?"
    Vernon Law/Pittsburgh Pirates (1950-51; 1954-67)

"I've never questioned the integrity of an umpire. Their eyesight, yes."
    Leo Durocher/ New York Giants Manager (1948-1955)

"Cheating is as much a part of the game as scorecards and hot dogs."
    Billy Martin/ Yankees Manager, (1975-79, 1983, 1985, 1988)

"I don't want to play golf. When I hit a ball, I want someone else to go chase it."
    Rogers Hornsby / St. Louis Cardinals (1915-1926)

Finally, the funniest saying, in my estimation from a pitcher I never heard about.

"I don't put any foreign substances on the baseball. Everything I use is from the good old U.S.A."
George Frazier / New York Yankees pitcher (1981-83)

It's Labor Day weekend and I am relaxing in my room at the "Changing Seasons" Motel on Route 5 near Lyndonville. There is a sports bar and lounge here and a lot of baseball paraphernalia on the walls. There is a red T-shirt with white lettering that says; "Will the woman who left nine children at Fenway Park please come and get them. They are beating the Yankees 5 to 0."

One day later. September 5th, 2010.

It is a rainy day Sunday here in beautiful Vermont where our sports thoughts may now turn to football since the Red Sox have played their way out of contention after losing both ends of a doubleheader to the White Sox. Manny Ramirez came to town and said nothing new. He is little more than an egotistical multi-millionaire who cares little for people, especially those below him. Does he belong in the Baseball Hall of Fame? I believe he belongs in the Baseball Hall of Shame. That doesn't exist yet but if it did, there would be plenty of candidates.

As I write this, Jonathan Papelbon has blown a save and the Chicago White Sox are about to take their third game in a row from the locals. They came home from a road trip and played disgustingly bad baseball. But, we stick with them and we love them still because they have provided us with two World Series championships since 2004 and as Joanne always told me. "Honey, you have to think positive."

I have things to do in the western United States. I have family to visit in beautiful Colorado and in California and in October, I plan to hold a memorial service for Joanne on the beach in Little River, California near where we used to live and we had so many good memories.

Acknowledgments

The grand old game of baseball is alive and well in America, despite the steroid issues. The ball park is still a delightful place to spend a day or an evening. I am so very proud to be acquainted with Bobby Doerr, Johnny Pesky and Bernie Carbo. Oh yes. Thank you, Dick Bresciani, the long time Vice President of Public Relations for the Red Sox. You opened the door to my dream and I am grateful.

Thanks so much to the Railroad Press in St. Johnsbury, Vermont for making my story a reality and thanks to all the nice people at Silver Mountain Graphics in St. Johnsbury.

I want to thank Johnny Pesky for asking if I knew anyone in California that would help me with the writing project. Of course I did. I called John Fremont of QED Press in Fort Bragg (not the military town). And next day, I had my credentials after Dick Bresciani had received a FAX from John. Now, I had my press credentials that would give me access to the green grass of Fenway, something I had imagined since the age of 10. I saw Johnny a lot during that 91 season when he was in uniform and hitting fly balls and grounders to the players before every game. I interviewed him at Fenway on a sunny day in June when Mo Vaughn came up from Pawtucket. I saw him again in 1992 when I returned to Winter Haven. Then Johnny was with me at Red Sox Fantasy Camp in 1994. He signed a baseball for me when I got my first hit in Ft. Myers against the pros. He sent me a Red Sox cap when I was recovering from cancer in 2002. I am so happy to see his number 6 up on the right field facade with the other Red Sox greats. The right field foul pole belongs to him. He is my friend and I love the guy.

The book is dedicated to Hall of Famer Bobby Doerr, # 1 in the hearts of Red Sox fans for many years. Thank you Bobby for being a guest on my radio program so many times and for regaling us with wonderful stories about your baseball career and your fishing exploits. God bless you, Bob Doerr. Bobby celebrates his 92nd birthday this coming April, 2011.

Kudos and many thanks go to my brother-in-law, Jan Hatch, for all the editing and suggestions that added heartfelt feelings to the story. A long time ago, Jan said; "The book isn't all about the Red Sox. It's about you and your life." That simple but correct observation changed the writing style. I began writing from my heart. I added "One Mans' Baseball Journey" to the title. Jan continues to work with me and Scott Beck of Railroad Street Press as we apply the finishing touches to what we believe will be a very enjoyable reading experience.

I want to thank Tom Brunansky for the first interview we did in Winter Haven and for being such a gracious guest so many mornings on the *Good New Guys* radio program. I spoke to Tom a few weeks ago to let him know the book was nearing completion. He said to be sure and let him know how to get a copy. Enjoy your golfing, Tom.

Thanks so much to Arnie and Winona Gadapee in Danville, Vermont, the prettiest town in New England. I've been to their house guest many times over the years and I'm grateful for their hospitality. Arnie and I were classmates. That class of 1954 at Danville High School was simply awesome. Rodney Daniels, Neil Randall, John Lapham, David Brock, "Stub" Parker, Herman Chamberlain, Gracia Emmons Berwyck, Marylene Fry Sevigny, Sylvia Hubbard, Barbara Greenwood and others are lifelong friends. We had some great teachers. They gave me some good writing skills. Special thanks go to Janet Hough Peduzzi of Montpelier (class of 53) for love and support over the years. Thanks to B.J. Murphy in St. Johnsbury for so many nice things he did for Joanne and me in 2010. Hey, Don Beattie. I'll see you and the other guys at the daily meetings this coming summer in St. Johnsbury.

I would be remiss if I didn't thank my dear friend and radio colleague, Jim Wagoner of Denver, Colorado. Jim and I earned our radio stripes working together at KDAC in Ft. Bragg. He and Dorothy continue to be a constant source of love and encouragement.

Words can hardly convey the love I feel for my west coast family; Joanne's three daughters, Lori, Marlene and Roberta and nine awesome grandchildren: Julia, Evan, Samantha, Heather, Jenna, Jeremy, Joshua, Jacob and the young girl that's growing up so fast, Jaci Marlo. Now, there are two great grandsons, Ely and Xavier. I am so blessed.

I'm writing from the comfort of my friends' home in Phoenix. I stopped here on the way to Florida and ended up in the hospital with a bout of pneumonia. Now, I'm facing surgery to repair and abdominal aortic aneurysm. Kelly McCall and her loving son, Ben, have opened their home to me and I am so grateful for their kindness. In 2007, Joanne and I were house sitters for Kelly while she went on a cross country ride from Seattle to Washington, D.C. on a bike she pedals with her hands. She's a remarkable lady.

My beautiful and extraordinarily talented wife, Joanne, holds a special place in my heart. The book would not have been completed without some gentle nudging from her. I miss her so much. Forty two days after Joanne's passing, I was involved in a horrendous accident at the Courtyard Marriott in Lebanon, New Hampshire. My foot slipped off the brake and on to the accelerator of my 2008 Dodge Ram Quad cab with camper shell. The truck shot forward like a rocket, then rolled down a 75 to 100 ft. embankment ending up on its wheels with the Hemi engine still running.. I was securely buckled to the driver's seat with only a small laceration on top of my head. The wooden urn with Joanne's remains was in my lap. My late wife saved my life. Somehow, by the grace of God, Joanne kept me from harm as the vehicle was rolling over at a tremendous rate of speed. I am so grateful to be alive. When my friend, Lauryn, the events coordinator heard what had happened out in the parking lot, she rushed to the Emergency Room at Dartmouth-Hitchcock Medical Center where they had taken me. Lauryn sat and held my hand for over an hour. I was encased in a cervical collar and could only stare at the ceiling while rejoicing at being alive. Thank you Lauryn and thanks to Ty Kulick and the entire front desk staff at the Marriott. After discharge from the ER, I came to the hotel in a hospital gown since my shirt had been cut away by the EMT's. Next morning, the staff found a nice long sleeved shirt for me, left behind by a guest.

Finally, thanks to Dan Shaughnessy and Nick Cafardo of the Boston Globe. What a pair of storytellers. They are always at the top of their game and I look forward to reading everything they write about the Red Sox this year.

The End

About the Author

Elmer "EJ" Barney divides his time between Vermont and northern California. He's part of a Hatch family on the West coast and a Hatch family on the East coast. In between, EJ spends time with his family in Colorado. From April to October, you'll find him in the heart of Red Sox country.

www.ingramcontent.com/pod-product-compliance
Lightning Source LLC
Chambersburg PA
CBHW051835090426
42736CB00011B/1813